ΔD Architectural Design

Fashion + Architecture

Compiled by Helen Castle

W·WILEY-ACADEMY

Architectural Design
Vol 70 No 6 December 2000

ISBN 0-471-49627-8
Profile No 148

Editorial Offices
International House
Ealing Broadway Centre
London W5 5DB
T: +44 (0)20 8326 3800
F: +44 (0)20 8326 3801
E: info@wiley.co.uk

Editor
Maggie Toy

Managing Editor
Helen Castle

Production
Mariangela Palazzi-Williams

Art Director
Christian Küsters ↘ CHK Design

Design Assistant
Owen Peyton Jones ↘ CHK Design

Freelance Assistant Editor
Corinne Masciocchi

Advertisement Sales
01243 843272

Photo Credits
ᗐ Architectural Design

Abbreviated positions
b=bottom, c=centre, l=left, r=right, t=top

P 4 © Richard Davies; p 6 courtesy Janson Goldstein, © Toshi Kawabata; pp 8, 9 & 10 © Jane Rendell; pp 12–13 © Michael Chittenden/Eric Kuhne and Associates; p 15(l) © Marks & Spencer; p 15(r) © Branson Coates Architecture, photos: Alastair Hunter; p 16 courtesy Sophie Hicks Architects, © Paul Smith Ltd, photos: Edina van der Wyck; p 17 © Claudio Silvestrin Architects Ltd; p 18 © BDP/Niall Clutton; p 19 © Checkland Kindleysides; p 20 © Paul Warchol Photography Inc; p 23(l) Ludwig Abache/Architectural Association; pp 24–27 courtesy Janson Goldstein, © Toshi Kawabata; pp 28–33 © Clive Sall; p 34(l) courtesy OMA/Rem Koolhaas, photo © Sanne Peper; p 34(r) courtesy OMA/Rem Koolhaas; pp 35, 36, 38 & 40 © Prada; p 42(l) courtesy Future Systems; p 42–43 © Jayne Merkel; p 44 © Foster and Partners/Ken Kirkwood; p 45(tl), 45(tr) & 45(cr) © Future Systems; 45(b) Hayes Davidson/Future Systems; p 46 © Richard Davies; 47(t) © Future Systems; 47(c) & 47(br) © Richard Davies; pp 48, 49, 50 & 51 Dennis Gilbert/View; portrait on p 49 courtesy B&B Italia, photo: Fabrizio Bergamo; p 52 courtesy Din Associates, © Jon O'Brien; p 52 portrait: courtesy Din Associates, photo: Louis Luislazo; p 53 © French Connection; p 54 courtesy Din Associates, © Jon O'Brien; p 55 courtesy Din Associates, © Jon O'Brien; pp 56–57 © Richard Davies; p 58(l) courtesy Wells Mackereth; p 58(r) and 59 courtesy Wells Mackereth, © Lewis Gasson; p 60 © Richard Davies; p 61 courtesy Wells Mackereth, © Gabrielle Shaw Communications/'Smiths' of Smithfield; p 62 courtesy Atelier Christian de Portzamparc, photos: © Nicolas Borel; p 64: courtesy Gluckman Mayner Architects, photo: © Lydia Gould Bessler; p 65 © Daniel Rowen Architect; p 66(t) © Paul Warchol Photograph Inc; pp 68–69 courtesy ShoP, © David Joseph; p 70 courtesy Donna Karan, New York, photos: © Todd Eberle; p 71(t) courtesy Antonio Citterio and Partners, photos Gionata Xerra; p 71(b) courtesy Lynn Herlihy and Dervyn Osbourne, Belmont Freeman Architects; p 72–73: courtesy Gluckman Mayner Architects, photo: © Lydia Gould Bessler; pp 74–75 © Paul Warchol Photography Inc; pp 76–77(t) © Paul Warchol Photography Inc; p 77(b) courtesy Toshiko Mori; p 78–79 courtesy Resnicow Schroeder Associates, photo: Masayui Hayashi; p 79 portrait: courtesy Resnicow Schroeder Associates, photo: Timothy Greenfield-Sanders; pp 80–81 courtesy Harvard University Graduate School of Design, © Liz Linder and Anita Kan; pp 82–83(t) courtesy Juan Salgado, photo: © Gunnar Knechtel; pp 82–83(b) photo: © Juan Salgado; p 84 (t) courtesy Juan Salgado, photo: © Gunnar

Knechtel; p 84(b) photo: © Juan Salgado; p 85(t) courtesy Juan Salgado, photo: © Gunnar Knechtel; pp 86–89 courtesy Mark Guard Architects, photos: Fernando Cordero and Joe Rank; main on p 90: courtesy Vexed Generation, Tony Doddle; p 90(tl), 90(tr) & 91(l) courtesy Vexed Generation, photo: Jonny Thompson; p 91(r) courtesy Vexed Generation, photo: Tom Howard; p 92(l) courtesy Egg, photo: Kenta Oki; p92(r) courtesy Egg, photo: Sebastian Gordan.

ᗐ+
P 95+ (t) courtesy Karen Franck, © Tomio Ohashi; p 95+ (b) courtesy Karen Franck, © Charlie Wolf; p 96+ courtesy Karen Franck, © Glynis Berry; 97+ (tl) & 97+ (tr) © Karen Franck; 97+ (b) courtesy Karen Franck, © Nils Ole-Lund; pp 99–102+ courtesy Martin Pearce and University of Portsmouth; p 103(t) courtesy Howard Tompkins Architects, © Evening Post, Jersey; p 103+ (b) © Haworth Tompkins Architects, photo: Andy Chopping; p 104+ (l) © Haworth Tompkins Architects, photo: Philip Vile; 104+ (r), 104+ & 106+ (l) © Haworth Tompkins Architects, photo: Andy Chopping; 106+(t) © Haworth Tompkins Architects; 106+ (bl) courtesy Haworth Tompkins Architects, photo: Andrew Putler; p 107 courtesy Haworth Tompkins, Hayes Davidson; p 108+ courtesy Haworth Tompkins, photos: Andy Chopping; p 111 © Steve Gartside.

Architectural Design would like to offer its apologies to Miles Glendinning and Stefan Muthesisus and the readers for the caption errors in The Transformable House, *ᗐ* (no 4, vol 70, 2000). The caption for the top right of p 29 should read: 'Mock-up prototype of 1953 for the LCC narrow-fronted maisonette type, designed by PJ Carter, AJ Colquhoun and C St John Wilson. The design is based on Le Corbusier's Maison Citrohan and Unité d'habitation in Marseilles, although the living room lacks Corbusier's double-height section.' The caption for p 31, placed at the bottom of p 30, should read: 'Plans for high flat blocks; all LCC, except first: Top left: Flats with balcony access at Churchill Gardens, Pimlico (Flats and Houses, 1958). Left: One and two-bedroom flats with corridor access (Flats and Houses, 1958). Top right: Point block with one at two-bedroom flats at Portsmouth Road, Alton East. Centre right: Point block with one and two-bedroom flats, Roehampton Lane, Alton West. Bottom right: Maisonettes and flats combined at Clive Street.' The caption for the top of p 33 should read: 'London: LCC "scissor" type; taking the idea of an indoor corridor between maisonettes from Le Corbusier, but complicating the pattern further by splitting the levels of the flats (eg Abbeyfield Road, Banner Street and Royal Victoria Yard or "Pepys").' The caption for the bottom of p 33 should read: 'Concrete Ltd "Bison Wall-Frame System", 1962. Only 21 parts were needed for one two-bedroom flat in a high block.'

Cover photograph:
© Dennis Gilbert/View.

Subscription Offices UK
John Wiley & Sons Ltd.
Journals Administration Department
1 Oaklands Way, Bognor Regis
West Sussex, PO22 9SA
T: +44 (0)1243 843272
F: +44 (0)1243 843232
E: cs-journals@wiley.co.uk

Subscription Offices USA and Canada
John Wiley & Sons Ltd.
Journals Administration Department
605 Third Avenue
New York, NY 10158
T: +1 212 850 6645
F: +1 212 850 6021
E: subinfo@wiley.com

Annual Subscription Rates 2000
Institutional Rate: UK £135
Personal Rate: UK £90
Student Rate: UK £60
Institutional Rate: US $225
Personal Rate: US $145
Student Rate: US $105

ᗐ is published bi-monthly.
Prices are for six issues and include postage and handling charges. Periodicals postage paid at Jamaica, NY 11431. Air freight and mailing in the USA by Publications Expediting Services Inc, 200 Meacham Avenue, Eimont, NY 11003

Single Issues UK: £19.99
Single Issues outside UK: US $32.50
Order two or more titles and postage is free. For orders of one title ad £2.00/US $5.00. To receive order by air please add £5.50/US $10.00

Postmaster
Send address changes to *ᗐ* c/o Expediting Services Inc, 200 Meacham Avenue, Long Island, NY 11003

Printed in Italy. All prices are subject to change without notice.
[ISSN: 0003-8504]

Fashion + Architecture
Compiled Helen Castle

Architectural Design +

Fashion and Architecture grew out of the conviction that something was afoot in the relationship between fashion and architecture. The initial inspiration for the title was a short column by Martin Pawley in 28 October 1999's *Architects' Journal*, in which he identified the emergence of a new culture in fashion, retail and architecture; a global culture dictated by the acquisition of elite fashion houses by retail conglomerates, who were quickly realising architecture's marketing and branding potential. As Pawley suggested, this all smacked of the 'sinister'.

Certainly, the cultural implications of increasing corporate control of private and public space is an unsettling prospect. As Dietmar Steiner suggests in his essay 'Promotional Architecture', there is the very real possibility that the overwhelming drive to sell consumables will render the architecture of cultural monuments, galleries and department stores almost indistinguishable. This process can already be observed in New York, the centre of the contemporary art market, where Jayne Merkel describes how fashion retail continually takes the initiative from commercial art galleries: emulating their design in their shops, shadowing their geographical location in the city and even incorporating exhibitions in their shop floors.

Ironically, all this has not had an adverse effect on fashion architecture itself. What seems to be on the cusp of emerging is a new generation of shops by architects, who are not only highly inventive and innovative in their formulation of strategic and design solutions, but canny and knowing in relation to corporate culture. They are perhaps best personified by Rem Koolhaas, who in his interview with Charles Jencks, openly admits to saying 'yes' to global culture as an architect reliant on commissions, while at the same time regarding consumerism in a 'nuanced way'. This new attitude among architects, combined with the commercial clamour in retail for design innovation fuelled by the onset of e-tail, has provided a path away from minimalism. As the predominant style in retail for over a decade minimalism was increasingly becoming a shackle to architects, in which they were repeatedly required by clients to reproduce the same finely detailed, overtly architectural spaces. In this light, perhaps the most exciting and brilliant retail solution is Future Systems' design concept for the Milanese company Marni. Rather than creating an entirely fixed solution, the stores are designed to accommodate the seasonal changes of the fashion collection - the floors float away from the walls, like an island, and the interior paintwork is intended to change in colour in accordance with the clothes. This can only be seen as an indication that architects are becoming more prepared to collaborate further in their work with the fashion industry rather than holding it forever at arm's length. *Helen Castle*

Opposite
Future Systems, interior of Marni, Sloane Street, London. Completed in the autumn of 2000, Future Systems' scheme for this Milanese-based fashion company marks a distinct departure in fashion retail. In contrast to the strictures of the now-accepted style of fashion architecture minimalism, it is designed to be flexible. Its interior decoration can be changed to shift with the seasonal collections of the fashion house.

Introduction **Martin Pawley**

Fashion and Architecture in the 21st Century

Last autumn, when the exhibition celebrating 25 years of the work of Giorgio Armani opened at New York's Guggenheim Museum, there was uproar. It was even claimed that Armani had made a $15 million donation to the Guggenheim Foundation 'in return for an opportunity to rewrite the history of fashion', as one newspaper tartly put it. Whatever the truth of the matter, Armani did score a notable first: the museum allowed his retrospective to occupy its architectural holy of holies, the Frank Lloyd Wright spiral gallery.

Architecture does not always figure as prominently in the status games of fashion as this, but it is frequently present in a supporting role. The Armani exhibition, for instance, was not designed by an architect, but it might as well have been. Out went the old Armani, famous for coaxing the males and females of the yuppie generation into a professional uniform that owed more to careful fabric research and factory production methods than traditional skills. In came the new Armani, no longer a name to sell sunglasses with, but a creator of fabulously expensive couture evening gowns for celebrities to wear.

In terms of the New York cultural *Zeitgeist* this was a cheque that could have bounced. That it didn't owed a lot to the inclusion of architecture in the equation. Anyone brave enough to question the barefaced rebranding of Giorgio Armani had to reckon not only with the status and reputation of the Guggenheim, but with the towering reputation of Frank Lloyd Wright.

Endorsement by association in this way is one of the things that architecture does best, and also one of the things that fashion, the industry, needs most – the new car parked outside the manor house, the classical revival office building, the corporate headquarters campus, the view from the castle, the minimalist interior ... All of them can be borrowed for a day or a week to make or remake a reputation, even when it is scarcely necessary — as was the case with the Norman Foster exhibition 'Exploring the City', which was almost contemporaneous with the Armani show. Like Armani's, Foster's show was held at an architectural place of worship – his own Sainsbury Centre for the Visual Arts at the University of East Anglia. But as with Armani's, his history too was 'updated' by emphasising recent urban master planning work at the expense of important early buildings.

Of course too much can easily be made of exhibitions as indicators: they are propaganda, displaying what their promoters and designers want us to know about a subject. Even so, in terms of the presence of a papered over past, the similarity of the Armani and Foster exhibitions is telling. At different times in their careers both these men did involve themselves deeply in the study of new materials and manufacturing methods, yet it is precisely this aspect of their work that the two exhibitions fail to emphasise. The chemistry of fabrics and the limits of machinery are of little interest to exhibitors or spectators. That is why the more an art or craft falls into the hands of advanced technology and specialist knowledge, the more its practitioners strive to compensate by presenting the object as the virgin birth of an individual genius.

It is by means of images, which are ubiquitous and relatively cheap, that fashion and architecture use one another, not simply as backdrops or celebrity head counts, but as guarantees of cultural acceptability. The traditional role of patronage – the commissioning or occupation of significant buildings – is now the preserve of the luxury retailers like lvmh, with its annual £5 billion turnover; or Condé Nast with its array of magazines. lvmh, which has a stable of once-independent brands including Dior, Givenchy, Lacroix and Loewe, also has its own Manhattan 'pocket skyscraper', designed by Christian de Portzamparc and located not far from Fox & Fowle's celebrated 'Green Skyscraper' leased by Condé Nast.

It is because images are the real currency of architecture, often outliving the structures they commemorate, no less than of fashion, where they are used in their millions, that both are so dependent on the traditional media of newspapers and magazines. This is particularly evident at the beginning of each season when fashion is on the march and every newspaper, magazine and colour supplement carries page after page of fashion news endlessly dotted with designer names. Despite repeated efforts, architecture has nothing to equal this. It too is dominated and valued according to names, but their advance is more discreet, never amounting to anything like the army of exotic models fashion can raise, marching towards the camera, identified only by names that tell the cognoscenti all they want to know. Apart from a handful of stars and one or two globalised design firms, the bulk of the profession of architecture is unknown to the general public. Instead a profession whose role was once defined as the three dimensional arrangement of solids and voids, has now shed much of its old simplicity in favour of a new half political, half technological status. Like famous names selling sunglasses internationally recognised architects now float above an occult mix of science and regulation like buoys above a diver. The work of their dedicated staff, devoted to the achievement of the enclosure of space by means of the thinnest and most translucent skin imaginable, taking place in conditions of submarine secrecy.

The similarity of their quest to that of the fashion designer is uncanny. Whereas only a decade ago dresses could be found with shapes of their own (and only a century ago dresses were nothing but shapes into which bodies were compressed), today's fashion is about bodies enclosed by the thinnest and most translucent skins, just like buildings. The essence of the common ground of architect and fashion designer is to be immersed in technicalities. The proof is their shared use of the same word 'fabric'.

Like unmanned spacecraft programmed to meet in orbit around some distant star, fashion in its search for newer and more diaphanous fabrics, and architecture in its search for more and more attenuated enclosures are destined to become one. When that day dawns the age of endorsement by association and the era of the tyranny of photography will finally be over. The establishment of a proper continuum between fashion and architecture make it possible for Giorgio Armani and Frank Lloyd Wright to share an exhibition space without complaint. ◠

Between Architecture, Fashion and Identity

Discussions of the relationship between fashion retail and architecture are inextricably entwined with political and theoretical attitudes to consumption. Whereas, for many years, the sale of goods was regarded by marxist commentators as no more than compensation for wage labour, shopping is now being seen as a proactive pursuit with a dynamic part to play in the formation of social and lifestyle identities. Here, Jane Rendell looks at how this approach is theoretically underpinned by the work of Walter Benjamin and Pierre Bourdieu. She also asks whether in an era of all-pervasive capitalism, it is possible for architects and artists to concurrently engage with, and be critical of, commodification.

itself are all acts determined by their context, they can serve only one purpose – to sell. This is a depressing scenario, where the architect/designer/ artist plays a passive role in the service of commodity capitalism. Indeed, an old-style marxist critique would take exactly this stance. However, in our western version of so-called democratic and liberal late capitalism, things are not that simple. It is no longer either/or – either we accept capitalism and live out our days drawing 1:1 shelving details for new branches of Ted Baker, or we reject capitalism and choose instead to flog a left-wing rag at a north London tube station on a Saturday morning. No, the situation is far more complex to negotiate.

At this point, it is useful to reflect on the work of two writers whose theories have been highly influential to discussions of consumption and architecture: Walter Benjamin on shopping arcades and Pierre Bourdieu on taste and 'distinction'. These writers are important, for they offer us two different ways of approaching this subject area. Following Benjamin, we can consider the relationship between architecture, fashion and identity in terms of everyday life, where the commodities we buy and the places in which we buy them are set within the context of popular culture. Following Bourdieu, we can explore both how architectural design can inform the purchase and use of commodities, while itself a commodity.

A couple of weeks ago, walking along Bond Street in London's West End, I noticed two women in the shop window of a designer-label fashion store. At first, I thought they were a couple of shop assistants taking a break from setting up the window display. On closer scrutiny, I noted their flawless make-up, manicures and carefully chosen outfits. Their occupation of the window space was incredibly self-conscious. On second thoughts, were they not intentionally, rather than unintentionally, in the window display? Real women as mannequins. Remember Tilda Swinton in a glass box in the Serpentine Gallery. Yet watching me watching them, they smiled. I smiled. This was a scene hard to define: was it an art installation, a window display or an everyday act of shop maintenance? The ambiguity of the moment sets up the discussion that follows, which explores the territory between architectur and fashion. I examine notions of the intentional and the accidental, display and consumption, art and shopping, popular culture and critical practice, using the work of Walter Benjamin and Pierre Bourdieu to define a more theoretical backdrop.

The place where architecture, fashion and identity come together is highly topical but also highly tricky. If the displaying of objects in a shop window, the designing of the window and the shop

In academic study, especially in disciplines such as anthropology, geography, art and architecture that are interested in material and spatial culture shopping is a socioeconomic activity that is becoming increasingly important. For many, especially those influenced by marxist theory, an interrogation of the sites, modes and social relationships of production has shifted to questioning those of consumption (see the number of publications produced in the mid-1990s on this topic). The most influential contributors to the debate are arguably Daniel Miller and Mary Douglas, and from a more obviously 'spatial' perspective, Rob Shields and John Urry whose work is groundbreaking in its discussions of the patterning of space through consuming.[1]

From the point of view of cultural studies it is possible, even desirable, to argue that consumption is itself a form of cultural production, but in architectural terms production has a distinct meaning: the design and physical construction of a building by an architect and a contractor for a client. In architecture, a shift from producing towards consuming has changed our understanding of the environment, resulting in a new focus on the ways in which buildings are used and experienced after completion. This perspective was certainly stressed by the *Strangely Familiar* contibutors and is also the primary concern of Jonathan Hill's recent edited collection.[2] We might call this area 'architecture and the everyday'.

Here, we must introduce Benjamin. In his work, activities and environments such as shopping and arcades are the subject of intellectual debate. His fascination with architecture was not as a series of isolated objects but in terms of a much larger project – the spaces of modernity. Thematically, for Benjamin, architecture was an image of the effects of capitalism. Methodologically, architecture was a dialectical image, a spatialised representation of a philosophical/historical idea. His study of architecture progressed through a series of city portraits – Naples, Berlin, Marseilles and, most famously, Paris.[3] The first essay, co-written with Asja Lacis, places Naples against the historical disintegration of the Roman Empire where the boundaries of public and private desired by capitalism are as yet unstructured. In this nascent state, architecture does not consist of a series of isolated and monumental objects in space. Rather outside, and inside are interwoven to create a city fabric where internal and external are experienced as complementary aspects of everyday life. The central idea here, that of 'porosity' – the dissolution of the inside-outside dichotomy – can be traced in his work on arcades.

Benjamin's major work was to have been a study of Paris focusing on the arcades as a miniature labyrinth within the larger labyrinth of the city. For him, the Parisian arcades were interpenetrations of public and private space, privately owned realms within the public zone. Benjamin's writings on the arcades, the things and the figures to be found within them, and the more abstract ideas they represent to him, such as dreams, myths, history and nature, suggest that for this philosopher architecture was but part of a much larger entity – life itself. Architecture is urban texture, a rich and complex composition of diverse objects, people and activities. Benjamin's work on arcades was never finished, but the fragments that exist compose a mosaic of short texts with titles

such as 'Fashion', 'Dolls', 'Flâneurs', 'Glass'. These pieces of prose continue to fascinate those studying urban culture and have had a remarkable effect on architectural criticism in a number of ways.

We have already mentioned how we might choose to study the space of popular culture rather than the intentionally designed one-off architectural object. Another effect of Benjamin's work on contemporary thinking has been to understand the city in terms of motion. Benjamin's interest in the poet Charles Baudelaire and the more generic figure of the urban flâneur strolling through the city offer a new model of urban experience.[4] The flâneur suggests that different sites may be connected through a mobile narrative, one that relies on the interrelation of place for its storyline rather than on a character-driven plot. Patrick Keiller's films *London* (1994) and *Robinson in Space* (1997) are examples of the ways in which we comprehend the city by walking through it. This is also a tendency expressed in current art practice and curatorship, where the city is the gallery and the artist operates as tour guide.[5]

Benjamin's 'working in fragments' has also been highly influential. According to him, every fact is already theory, even at a microlevel. From design detail to Barbie doll, the things around us tell something of the larger issues at stake. Certainly, for writer Patrick Wright and artist Richard Wentworth, mundane objects and places in the city, from telephone box to wooden spoon, open up a world of critical and political commentary on urban history and modern life. It is this aspect of Benjamin's work, this consideration of architecture as integral to everyday life, that is important to contemporary discussions about the importance of architecture, fashion and the role of consumption in constructing identity.

Shopping is a complex weave of a number of different spatial practices that include displaying, exchanging and consuming. Consumption - the selection and acquisition of goods - is not only a simple economic act of buying and selling. It also has a symbolic function – goods represent social values. In traditional marxist critique, consumption is merely a compensation for alienated wage labour and, as such, it is a passive activity. But recent work discusses the important and proactive role that consumption plays in the formation of identity.[6] By choosing and buying certain goods, the consumer identifies him/herself with a status, lifestyle or social identity. However much Marx we have or haven't read, most of us, at one time or another, have taken some delight in shopping, even if it is only for a good cup of coffee at the station.

It is worth considering how consumer goods communicate cultural meaning through social rituals – acquisition, possession, exchange, grooming and divestment. Pierre Bourdieu's work is important here. According to Bourdieu, the social construction of

Notes
1. See Daniel Miller (ed),
Acknowledging Consumption,
Routledge (London), 1995; Rob
Shields (ed), Lifestyle Shopping,
Routledge (London), 1992;
John Urry, Consuming Places,
Routledge (London), 1995.
2. Jonathan Hill (ed), Occupying
Architecture: Between the
Architect and the User,
(Routledge), London, 1998.
3. Walter Benjamin, One Way
Street and Other Writings,
Verso (London), 1992.
4. Walter Benjamin, Charles
Baudelaire: a Lyric Poet in the
Era of High Capitalism, Verso
(London), 1997.
5. See for example the audio
tours of Janet Cardiff and
Bures Miller commissioned
by the Louisiana Museum
(1996), Skulpture. Projekts
in Munster (1997), and the
Whitechapel Gallery in
London's East End (1999).
6. See Iain Borden, Joe Kerr,
Alicia Pivaro, Jane Rendell
(eds), Strangely Familiar:
Narratives of Architecture in
the City, Routledge (London),
1995; Borden, Kerr, Rendell
(eds) with Alicia Pivaro, The
Unknown City: Contesting
Architecture and Social
Space, MIT (London), 2000.
7. Pierre Bourdieu, Distinction:
a Social Critique of the
Judgement of Taste, Routledge
Kegan Paul (London), 1984.
8. Kathy Battista, 'The Art of
Shopping: Salon 3 and Saks
5th Avenue', in Jane Rendell
(ed), 'A Place Between', Public
Art Journal, No 2, October 1999.

Jane Rendell is lecturer in
architecture at University
College London. An
architectural designer, historian
and theorist, she is author of
the forthcoming The Pursuit of
Pleasure (Athlone Press). She is
also editor of 'A Place Between',
Public Art Journal, No 2,
October 1999, and has co-edited
a number of publications.

lifestyles and consumption patterns can be explained through the social dynamics of negative distinction.[7] He highlights the role that strategies of distinction play in allowing ever more subtle variations in taste to be articulated. Distinctions are created not just through buying more goods, but by playing with an existing 'vocabulary' of material signs through the development of a 'rhetoric' of use. Performing consumption plays a key role in the construction of distinct and fashionable identities. It is in the 'acting out' of shopping in and through architecture, and the 'acting out' of the purchase and use of architecture, that identities are continually constructed and reconstructed. Indeed, Bourdieu argues that the display of status symbols is as important as their possession. As magazines like Wallpaper* make perfectly clear, it is only in the combining of places – shop, home, work place and play space – and in the juxtaposing of things – dresses, forks, computers and bricks – that we fully articulate who we like to think we are. And time is important. There are the times and places of consideration and deliberation, of desire before consummation; and there are the periods and environments occupied postpurchase, where products are displayed and enacted through use. It is fashionable to know exactly how and when to place the kitsch against the minimal. Increasingly, it is not only the goods bought in shops that say something about who we are, or would like to be, but also the design of the shops themselves. And as the success of practitioners such as Branson Coates, FAT and others have made clear, it is not those architects who are passive, but rather those who challenge the status quo, who delight in being on the edge, who are the most in demand. By being a bit 'different', they are able to create a distinct site and identity for a product. But the role of the 'radical' architect in the world of retail requires a certain degree of complicity. It is hard to control the effect of the 'difficult' position. An act of resistance is possible at any moment. By providing a memorable place, architecture enhances product identity, but is itself commodified.

The role of architecture as a commodity is of growing interest. The kind of architecture we commission, buy and occupy can indicate our real and aspirational position in relation to others. The design of space can represent differences between people in terms of their income, sexual preferences, cultural backgrounds and ages, and allow the continually evolving cross-referring between these rather reductive categories to be made manifest, creating multiple and fluid identities.

The use of architecture in identifying 'cultural capital' is manifest in Bilbao's Guggenheim Museum and Walsall's New Art Gallery for example. Both buildings have put their cities on the cultural map. And the purchase of these architectural commodities has been worth it. These pieces of architecture have redefined the value of their contexts in a dramatic way. In Bilbao, the choice of such a 'named' and maverick architect as Frank Gehry greatly helped to create a public profile. In Walsall, the lesser known architectural practice of Caruso St John has become unexpectedly familiar. But it is not all media hype. Both buildings are enjoyed by art and architectural critics and welcomed by the local residents precisely because they are different.

Is it possible for art and architecture to engage closely with commodification and remain critical of it? From the Frankfurt School to Jake and Dinos Chapman, we have come a long way. It is not about choosing high or low culture, shopping or art/architecture, but about negotiating the area between – the hybrid. In architectural academia, the themed casinos of the Las Vegas strip have become the new cool in radical debate. In the recent Comme des Garçons in Chelsea, New York – a district dominated by contemporary art galleries – the fit of two elite cultures is seamless. Articles of clothing are art objects in a silent and hallowed space. The selling of clothing, as in most designer outlets, has happily taken on the rules of the gallery: look don't touch. The hybrids here hold no tension. Academia claims the popular. Architecture creates an elite environment for designer fashion – the gallery.

When architects and artists are commissioned by developers to make spaces to sell products, is it possible for critical practice to result? When academics decide to think about shopping, is it possible for 'everyday' life to resist?

In a recent article in the Public Art Journal, Kathy Battista discussed two projects that talk more about the tensions of such intersections of art/architecture and shopping.[8] In the first, where a young group of curators, Salon 31, turned a disused shopping unit in south London's Elephant and Castle shopping centre into a space for emerging artists, the worry is that the viewing rules of the imported gallery may colonise shopping-mall context. In the second, where contemporary artists created displays in the shop windows of Saks, Fifth Avenue, New York, we ask whether critical aspects of an artist's work can withstand the commodifying tendencies of the context. In both cases, there is ambiguity. With no immediate or obvious alternatives to commodity capitalism, the ambiguous is the critical frontline. ∆

Fashioning

Architectural Tactics
and Identity Statements

Iain Borden takes us on a shopping spree through the controlled concourses of Bluewater shopping mall to the less predictable variety of stores in the metropolis beyond. For him, the true relationship between fashion and architecture lies not in set piece store designs, but in the differences struck up between shops, with their individual wares, in the greater urban context.

the City

Eric Kuhne & Associates,
Bluewater, Kent. Built in
1999, this shopping centre
is the biggest in the UK,
if not Europe.

Let me begin with a fashion nightmare masquerading as a retail dream. Bluewater, the mega-mall shopping complex in Kent, is an experiment in consumerism – a £375 million, 240 acre, self-contained world replete not only with 1.5 million square feet of lettable space spread over 325 fashion shops and other retail outlets, not only with six individualised mall strips on two levels, not only with ample parking for all, but also with three full-blown leisure villages offering multiscreen cinemas, outdoor plazas, food courts, night-time bars, public art works and a rock-climbing wall. This is the Utopia of late capitalism, a place where all that is troublesome in the city is erased, where there are no homeless people, wailing sirens or speeding couriers, but where there is always, with absolute 100 per cent certainty, a place to sit down, a drink to be quaffed, a toilet to be found and a new product to be purchased. This is what Bluewater's managers call 'retailment' (a neologism born from retail + entertainment), 'a whole experience' that promises to 'integrate retail and leisure in a new way, and enhance both the guest's experience and the retailers' performance'. This is contented consumerism where the visitor is always relaxed enough to open their wallet (hence enhancing 'retail performance'), and always happy to be a citizen through shopping (hence the term 'guest' rather than shopper or consumer).

depictions of the River Thames, cornices are decorated with representational friezes and poetic inscriptions, and the three corner-hubs contain thematised installations relating to the moon, tides and other such uplifting conceptual armatures. This is what master architects Eric Kuhnes Associates call 'architectural diversity'.

Given this degree of architectural effort, it is hard to fault Bluewater – it is undoubtedly one of the best shopping malls of its kind. If in need of a new shirt or pair of shoes, this would be a fine place to go. Or would it? For while Bluewater is of very good quality, it is very-good-quality false consciousness – an ideological palace that pretends to be a city, but in fact has none of the more unstable properties that cities really offer. It is an internalised, predictable, controlled, safe and sterile arena in which there is an asymmetry of power between the managers (the mall operators) and the managed (the shoppers).

In the realm of fashion and architecture this is particularly problematic, for in shopping for clothes one is above all searching for a sense of one's own identity, for a layer in which to drape one's self-image in relation to the city outside. Bluewater offers none of this beyond the products themselves, beyond the homogeneity of predictable goods in routine spaces. So how do fashion and architecture interact outside of the Bluewater nightmare? How does one avoid the anxiety so perfectly expressed by The Clash: 'I'm all lost in the supermarket/Can no longer shop happily/Came in here for the special offer/Guaranteed personality'?

'I'm all lost in the supermarket Can no longer shop happily Came in here for the special offer Guaranteed personality'

It is not, however, just the impressive list of facilities that produces the mood of calm and continuous spending. It is also the quality of the architecture, for Bluewater proudly displays an artful blend of wide concourses, marbled surfaces, historical styles, large sculptures, variegated colours and playful light. Barrel-vaulted roofs are interspersed with splendorous arched windows and centred oculi, floors proffer

It is the differentiation of the city that is most important – a sense that in wandering and interacting with others one may find another new space, shop or item. The relationship between fashion and architecture in the city is, then, not about anticommodification (that is not what is wrong with Bluewater, for all fashion shops sell clothes as exchange value), but is, or should be, about antihomogenisation. Urbanism means multiplicity – not the (false) multiplicity within one

bounded place like Bluewater, but the possibility of true multiplicity in the city as a totality. And therefore the interaction between fashion and architecture is, or should be, about this variation, about finding different ways to mediate the relationship between self, clothing, place of purchase and urban context as a whole.

Vive la Difference

Fashion shops can make a difference – and not just the difference of new clothing items offering a subtle modification to the range already on offer (a daring buckle here, an odd lapel detail there). Shops can profoundly shift not only the way people dress but also the way in which they treat the city. Such places are, by nature, few and far between, but chief among them must be Sex, the shop on London's King's Road opened by Malcolm McLaren and Vivienne Westwood in the 1970s, which became the ephemeral centre of the burgeoning punk scene and fed the aggressive imagery of zips and pins, blacks and reds, slogans and motifs, found items and collided styles that has fuelled so much street-wise fashion ever since. The architectural legacy of Sex is found in the plethora of challenging fashion shops dotted around metropolises everywhere – shops with strange names and impenetrable displays, which dare you to enter within. Albeit with few of Sex's countercultural references, devices like the recent Future Systems' monocoque aluminium tunnel entrance to the Comme des Garçons store in New York (where the original external rough brickwork, signage and fire escape are untouched), or even the mid-1980s Norman Foster steel and glass bridge into the Katherine Hamnett store (located in an old car-body repair shed), also imply that they unlock strange worlds. These architectures suggest that, should you care to experience them, you may be transformed into something different from the person you know.

Homeliness

The exact opposite is the intense normalcy projected by Marks & Spencer, where an expanse of clear glass and a line of gently swinging doors allow you to peer in from the pavement, to check that there is nothing strange whatsoever about the world inside. Once across the portal, a palette of calm browns, greys and greens with the occasional flash of brass and chrome reassures you further that everything here is predictable and reliable – this in an architecture for plain white cotton T-shirts and sensible skirts, and for making exotic Italian

Above left
Marks & Spencer stores project a homely, familiar image, which is reassuring for customers.

Above right
Branson Coates, Katherine Hamnett, Sloane Street, 1988. With fish tanks in the window, Nigel Coates' shop – now replaced by a pared-down space by Chipperfield – epitomised high-camp, theatrical style.

foods and silk lingerie seem contained, familiar, packaged. It is an architecture in which to feel at home.

Globalism

Playing a dangerously similar game are chains like Benetton and The Gap, who must also seem predictable and safe while simultaneously mixing a whiff of cosmopolitan internationalism with the scent of youth. These architectures are curiously close to Marks & Spencer, with the same formula of simple materials and brightish lighting, but in smaller stores and with carefully positioned graphics. It is these graphics that disclose the real nature of Gap/Benetton architecture, which is never contained within any single store but is dispersed globally, like the brand, through hundreds of other such stores in cities worldwide, and, just as importantly, through hundreds of thousands of advertisements on television, billboards and Formula One cars. Each time you enter the store of Gap/Benetton, you are also entering, by mediated association, their geographic world: Los Angeles, Milan, Tokyo, Sao Paulo, Berlin, Jakarta, Sydney, Monaco ...

City Quarter

If Gap/Benetton fashion architecture suggests a peripatetic, international youth class, just one Go flight away from another cool city, then the City Quarter offers an equivalent but more local experience. Whether it is Scheunenviertel in Berlin or Nolita in New York (north of Little Italy), a newly fashionable part of town becomes one in which to cruise and get lost a little, on the lookout not for fashion stores that you know, but for those you do not; one where a system of looks is set up between yourself, others doing the same, and the network of streets and stores that binds you loosely together. This is the architecture of the unknown, of the promise of a new discovery.

The Other

Nor does this quarter have to be predominantly known for its fashion. Every city has its flea markets, jumble sales, car-boot sales, street markets and ethnic markets, where the idiosyncratic *fashionista* seek out leather jackets, combat trousers, a yard or two of impossibly bright silk, old hats ... Here, the architecture is strictly whatever comes with the territory: rusty-wheeled street stall, run-down yet packed-to-the-ceiling terraced shop, grim village hall open every third Sunday of the month, or an estate-car rear door held horizontal over asphalted playground. These architectures are rarely connected with clothing, still less with fashion, and are all the more seductive for it.

Narrative

There is, of course, also the condensed version of the City Quarter and The Other, a place where city hybridity is condensed into a hot coalition of styles, moods and colours. While Philippe Starck creates the pseudo-ambience of a Savile Row tailor-cum-gentleman's club for Hugo Boss in Paris, or designers like Din Associates resort to such things as an aquarium and porthole motif for a shoe store within Harrods, others structure the narrative deep within their designs. At the shop-in-a-house store for Paul Smith in Westbourne Grove, Sophie Hicks Architects combine thematised rooms (Play Room for children, Archer Room for men's informal, Kensington Room for women) with domestic shelving, trompe l'oeil murals, picture frames, freestanding wardrobes and a small landscaped garden. The pre-eminent and most extreme exemplars of the narrative tradition remain Branson Coates' store designs for Jigsaw and Katherine Hamnett. Here, theatrical collections of extravagant decorations, fabrics, chandeliers and mirrors are combined with sequential spatial devices like sunken gardens, curved staircases and spiral ceilings – setting up a stage of catwalks on which to parade, posture and pretend. This architecture is a fantasy world of punk-meets-Arabia, where you can preprogramme and prestyle yourself in advance of a later presentation to other city dwellers.

Blankness

For those of a less demonstrative and searching character, another fashion architecture offers cool restraint and minimal gesture. These are shops meticulously formulated from shadow-gap walls, concrete benches, sandblasted glass, stone or high-tech staircases and square-section metal shelves, creating an aura of permanence against the relative ephemerality of a few beautifully folded clothes and the occasional theatrical prop. Examples are now so legion that they verge on the new orthodoxy: Stanton Williams for Issey Miyake; John Pawson for Jigsaw, Calvin Klein and RK RK; Eva Jiricna for Joseph; Michael Gabelline for Jil Sanders and Nicole Farhi; David Chipperfield for Equipment, Joseph and Dolce & Gabbana; Peter Marino for DKNY ... In the case of Claudio Silvestrin for Giorgio Armani in Paris, the monastery that once occupied the Place Vendôme site is recalled in Silvestrin's typically austere minimalism: simple rectilinear floor plans and a palette of pale limestone, oxidised brass, African ebony and muted lights. This is architecture for those who do not feel the need to ask questions, be they about materials, prices or cleaning instructions: hence the blank walls, blank windows, blank price-tags. The message is contained not in extrovert logos, symbols or shapes, but in the poetic efficiency of subtle textures, shades and cuts. If this architecture speaks at all, it is in a gentle whisper.

This page
Sophie Hicks Architects, Paul Smith, Westbourne House, Westbourne Grove, London (1998). This Paul Smith store in a London town house is themed as a dwelling. The women's room has the relaxed atmosphere of a serene boudoir, with fresh white walls and a large bay window.

Opposite
Claudio Silvestrin, Giorgio Armani, Place Vendôme, Paris, 2000. The monastery that once occupied the site is recalled in Silvestrin's restrained interior.

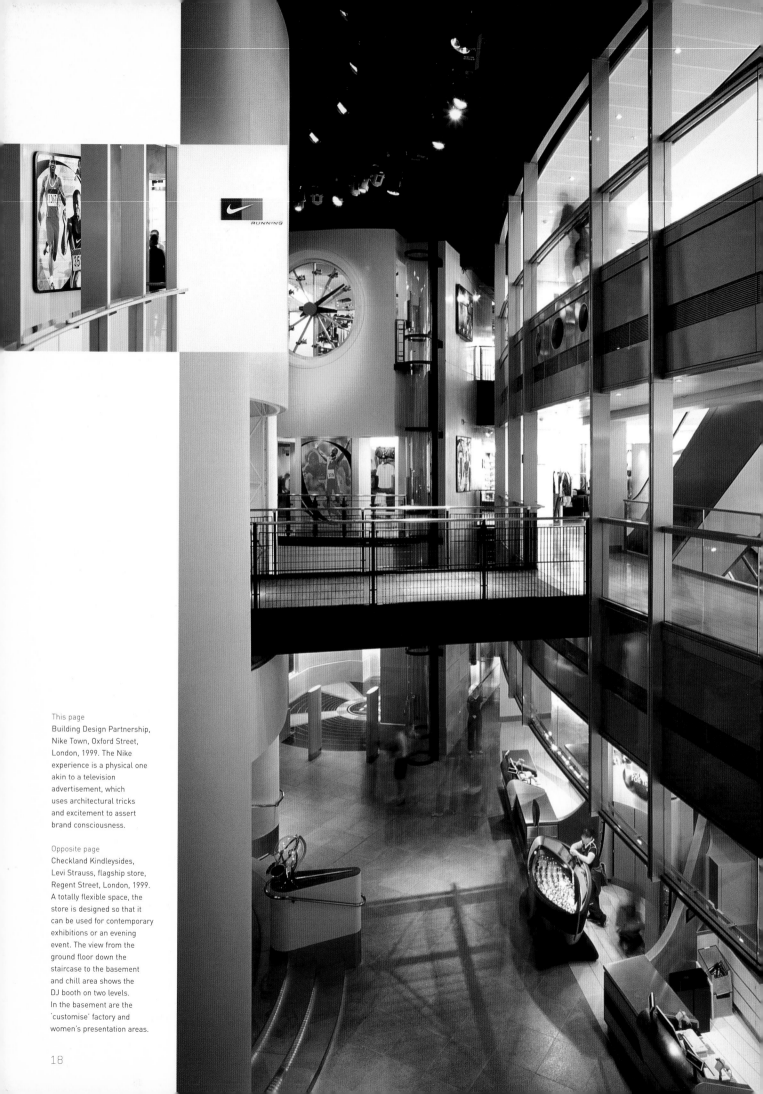

This page
Building Design Partnership,
Nike Town, Oxford Street,
London, 1999. The Nike
experience is a physical one
akin to a television
advertisement, which
uses architectural tricks
and excitement to assert
brand consciousness.

Opposite page
Checkland Kindleysides,
Levi Strauss, flagship store,
Regent Street, London, 1999.
A totally flexible space, the
store is designed so that it
can be used for contemporary
exhibitions or an evening
event. The view from the
ground floor down the
staircase to the basement
and chill area shows the
DJ booth on two levels.
In the basement are the
'customise' factory and
women's presentation areas.

Off-Balance

There are, however, few of us who communicate in such calm and centred tones. I too like to enter the blank world of minimal fashions, but it is only one of the worlds with which I associate - an attitude that stems directly from a culture of displacement, where the city dweller feels neither bourgeois nor proletarian, but is decentred among different groups and relationships. Shops like those for Stussy, the former skateboard clothing manufacturer turned off-high-street retailer, plug into this realm, using tilted plywood surfaces, street furniture and harsh materials (rough concrete walls, metal benches) to recall the street-savvy world of skateboarding without directly representing it (no skateboards on the walls, no skate videos playing in the corner). Such shops are directed not at the subcultural tribe (as Sex was at punks), but at those who desire short-term and multiple memberships in the city. Add these to your personal collage of urban experiences and self-identities.

Heritage

In this city of postmodern and hybrid cultures, do not forget that social associations can occur in time as well as in space. Although perhaps not part of the *GQ*, *Elle* or *Vogue*-reading itinerary, there are always those fashion stores that mine the power of historical association. Liberty, Laura Ashley, Past Times – these stores install themselves in old architecture (or in buildings that look old), to sell scarves, hats and cuff links – anything that can take a William Morris pattern or neo-Celtic motif. These are architectures by which to escape the modern world or, rather, become a person who is at once contemporary yet historically aware – interiors, that is, for heritage tourists.

Shops Without Shopping

Multiple memberships are not the sole preserve of countercultural or heritage-fashion outlets.

Places like Top Shop seek to entertain with table-football games, catwalk shows and plasma screens, while Levi Strauss employed Checkland Kindleysides for its flagship Regent Street store, where food store and nightclub rhetorics are recalled in 'chiller cabinets' and industrialised display shelves. Constant loud music signifies the fact that once a month the whole Levi store is turned into a bona fide club, so it is no surprise to see a double-turntable DJ booth looming at the rear. Nike, too, would like you to pursue a membership of its world – the sports world, that is, of Nike and all it sponsors. Nike Town is, as a consequence, a fashion shop where you are sold very little – it is an experience, a place to encounter the world of Nike, to feel empathy with the world of Nike, and only implicitly to purchase something from the world of Nike. In essence, this is fashion shop as excited advertisement, where vertiginous staircases, complex floor plates, explosive sounds and serial video screens are brought together to insert brand consciousness into the urban masses. And, when we have finally made a Nike purchase some time later, as we all inevitably will do, we each become mobile Nike Towns, proudly yet discreetly wearing the 'swoosh' stripe on our feet, torsos, chests or wrists.

Here, we are partially returned to the world of Bluewater – confident and smiling, made complete through the right commodity purchase, a state displayed on our bodies as we circumnavigate the city. Yet at least Nike Town demands that we enter that city, that we move around and encounter the unexpected as well as the predicted, that we at least allow for the possibility of doing something different today. As such, Nike Town perhaps best demonstrates the paradox of fashion consumerism, self and the city: the search for difference within a sea of homogeneity, for self-expression among a welter of standardised products, for a corporeal body among a world of data-images and messages. As much as one might dislike Nike Town, as personally I do, at least it allows for that paradox to be expressed. And here there is indeed clear blue water between, on the one hand, Nike Town and the other fashion stores of the city, and, on the other, the far-away world of the internalised mega-mall. ⌂

Iain Borden is Director of Architectural History and Theory at The Bartlett, University College London, where he is Reader in Architecture and Urban Culture. He is co-editor of *Architecture and the Sites of History* (1995), *Strangely Familiar* (1996), *The Unknown City* (2000), *Gender Space Architecture* (2000), *The City Cultures Reader* (2000), and *InterSections* (2000). He is the author of *Skateboarding, Space and the City: Architecture and the Body* (2001) and with Jane Rendell, of *DoubleDecker: Architecture through History, Politics and Poetics* (both forthcoming).

PROMOTIONAL ARCHITECTURE

I CAN'T TELL YOU

Is it a Cathedral, a Museum, or a Shop?

As they all conflate into promotional architecture, cultural monuments, galleries and department stores are becoming indistinguishable. Museums now sell as much as they show, creating places in which lifestyles are staged. In turn, fashion retail spaces are becoming chapels to consumerism and famous buildings are backdrops for commercials, fashion shoots and music videos. Dietmar M Steiner discusses how architects and their buildings are being absorbed into the ever-expanding world of corporate culture.

Scene one: Museum Guggenheim-SoHo, New York, 1998. The museum is showing a large exhibition of French postwar art. The till for tickets can be reached only after passing through the famous Guggenheim museum-shop – a shop as big as the Dean & Deluca delicatessen across the street. An exhibition of sculptures starts in the entrance lobby. Small objects are presented on waist-high pedestals. There is excitement at the cash desk. A customer of the shop, or maybe he is a visitor to the museum, has taken one of the small sculptures from the pedestal and wants to buy it. His mistake is explained to him.

Scene two: Not far away from the Guggenheim-SoHo is the New York shop of the fashion designer Helmut Lang. In the interior is an installation consisting of serial hermetic cubes. They could have been made by Donald Judd. Their open backs, however, reveal selected clothes, themselves presented like works of art. Next to the cash desk is a digital display of moving words. It looks like an installation by Jenny Holzer, but, not falling into the same kind of trap as the man in the Guggenheim-SoHo, we know it must be an advertising display for Helmut Lang. Or must it? No: the installation has indeed been created by Holzer.

Scene three: Museum Guggenheim-SoHo, New York, 2000. The Guggenheim museum-shop still exists, but the exhibition spaces have been rented out to the fashion firm Prada.

These are scenes observed in the world of architecture, arts and fashion; scenes with no clear-cut dividing lines; scenes of a changing assignation of values. During the past decade, a cultural shift as strange as it is interesting has taken place. The museum has become the ultimate building task in postmodern development. In the early stages of this shift, museums were characterised as the new cathedrals of society, based on the theatrical power of architecture. Frank Gehry, for example, stated that his Guggenheim Museum in Bilbao never would have come into being if Hans Hollein's Museum Abteiberg in Mönchengladbach had not released the power of the spectacle in the 1970s. In other words, there has been a belief that works of art can be framed and staged by architecture. Today, however, one only has to look at the examples above to see that this evaluation has shifted. Museums, by virtue of their architectonic conciseness, have become places where lifestyles are staged. This potential has been extended from the field of the arts and the museum to the field of fashion and advertising.

Thus, it is now becoming difficult to differentiate between a museum and a department store. In the design of the underground entrance floor of the Louvre, for example, the areas of cultural and commercial use are indistinguishable. While visiting a temple of fashion, on the other hand, one must be sunk in the silent humility of cultural devotion. This near-sacred architectural ambience can be found in the Calvin Klein flagship stores (Tokyo, Seoul, New York, Paris) of British Minimalist architect John Pawson, where each act of buying resembles a rite of confession and redemption. The shop assistants are untouchable ascetic priestesses, who graciously return one's credit card as if delivering the Host after the consecration, enforcing one's sense of belonging to the faithful brotherhood.

The boutique as a chapel of consumerism; fashion as an object of worship; the museum as department store: definitions are beginning to shift and functions are changing. The question is, what is the role of architecture in this process?

To begin to answer this question, a myth of Modernism must be exploded. Contrary to popular belief, Modernism, and every other 'style' prior to it, has always been an expression of lifestyle and fashion. This must have been the case, since otherwise the agreements and codes of society could not have attached themselves to it. When Le Corbusier photographed his houses, he carefully selected the appropriate cars to be placed in front of them. Of course, the Bauhaus, and the WChUTEMAS in the Soviet Union, brought architecture, art, design and fashion into an aesthetic balance. Only when the architectural history of Modernism was infiltrated by the categories of fine art, did the term 'fashion' become unacceptable, and architecture was expected to document a striving for truth and honesty, for progress and enlightenment. As a result, only very rarely were architectural achievements seen in a wider cultural context, which naturally, would have embraced fashion and everyday life.

The change in this attitude is commonly seen to have been produced by Postmodernism, not through its references to architectural history, but because of its openness to the phenomena of everyday life. Venturi/Scott-Brown/Izenour with *Learning from Las Vegas* (1972) opened up views on architecture as well as rediscovering the effect of aesthetics in American shops and the hotels of Morris Lapidus. However, the avant-garde of the 1960s had already left the internal architectural discussion behind, focusing instead on popular culture. Archigram, Coop Himmelblau, Haus-Rucker-Co and others were the first to use the marketing instruments of the mass media in order to communicate their ideas. But the basis was always the architectural evocation of atmosphere and appropriate ambience, the creation of products and symbols that could compete with a general world of goods.

In the 1980s and 1990s, there were signs of a new 'dialogue' between architecture and the market, or rather, between architecture and lifestyle. The set of Adrian Lyne's film *Nine 1/2 Weeks* (1985) set the tone for the cool Manhattan lofts with their venetian blinds and stylish lighting that would characterise the architecture of this period. Kim Basinger and Mickey Rourke hang out in Rei Kawakubo's Manhattan Comme des Garçons and bourgeois shops like the department store Bergdorf + Goodman. The following year, in the opening sequence of *The Big Easy* (Jim McBride, 1986) a corpse turns up in Charles Moore's Piazza d'Italia in New Orleans. With astonishing logic, Lieutenant Remy McSwain (Dennis Quaid) therefore concludes that this could only have been a Mafia murder (a conclusion, by the way, that was far off the mark). In a classic piece of product placement at the end of the same film, an apparently completely superfluous piece of equipment in the form of a small Apple-Macintosh SE sits decoratively on a desk.

When the film industry utilises new sites of architecture for its imagery, the glorification of the architects themselves cannot not be far away. The ongoing phenomenon of the 'star architect' endows certain individuals with enough celebrity to embark on other fields of activity. Sir Norman Foster advertises Rolex watches, for example, while Michael Graves promotes shoes. Disney also discovered the power of star architects like Graves, Aldo Rossi, Arata Isozaki, Robert M Stern, Frank Gehry etc, as a marketing instrument for its hotels, office buildings and recreational outlets.

The period that Jacques Herzog once called the epoch of grey and brown managers was over. He was referring to the grey-suited managers of the 1960s, who demanded a grey architecture in which to conduct their business, and to the 1970s when managers began to wear brown corduroy suits and flowered ties with bright shirts, leading to a more colourful and noisy architecture.

Today, corporate architecture has splintered into various individual identities, which turn up everywhere in the world. Branches of McDonald's are identical wherever they appear, representing, as Laurie Anderson once put it, 'everywhere a feeling of home'. Chainstores like Benetton, Body Shop, Esprit etc, springing up in all major international cities, have created a similar familiarity with their corporate designs.

Fashion empires, too, have moved into a corporate culture. They have become lifestyle producers, able to deliver the whole package. However, it is interesting that consumers very rarely buy everything from one company, never sticking to a single trademark but happily mixing different brands. As a result, fashion firms, especially in Milan, have become active in the field of urban development, building on Donna Karan's idea, which was to create a gigantic DKNY fire wall, now one of the most frequently photographed landmarks in Manhattan. In Milan, Missoni and Armani advertise on gigantic billboards featuring beamingly artificial models, which, surprisingly, offer more orientation within the city than any architecture.

In such a permanently expanding world of corporate culture and design, what is left over for architecture? In Europe, at least, there is housing, and educational or cultural buildings. But one has to be careful. So-called 'public' or 'social' housing is also expected to undergo a liberalisation and opening-up of markets. This will increasingly produce a popular component not unlike the American model of the new urbanism. Educational and cultural buildings only seem to be architecturally autonomous. In fact, they follow the market laws of public attention on a higher level. The proud report from Bilbao is that the additional revenues earned in the tourism industry has increased tax revenue to a level at which it has paid off the Basque government's costs for Gehry's Guggenheim Museum after three years. This building, which was not constructed to last for ever, could therefore follow the rules of the tourist industry and be left to fall into ruins if its economic return on capital comes to an end. Meanwhile, the trustees of the Tugendhat House by Mies van der Rohe

Dietmar M Steiner studied architecture at the Academy of Fine Arts in Vienna. He now works as an architectural historian, theoretician and critic. He has taught at the Institute of History and Theory of Architecture at the Academy of Applied Arts in Vienna. From 1995 to 1999, he was Architectural Editor of *Domus*. Since 1993, he has been the Director of the Architecture Centre, Vienna. He is on the board of the ICAM (International Confederation of Architecture Museums) and of the advisory committee for the 'Mies van der Rohe Pavilion Prize', the European Prize for Architecture.

This text was translated from the German by Barbara Schmiedeknecht.

in Brno are taking the opposite approach, hiring the villa out as a location for TV commercials in order to finance its renovation.

Of course, the Guggenheim Museum – signalling 'spectacle' – has been used as a location in several advertising campaigns. But who would have expected that a quiet, remote building like Peter Zumthor's bath in Vals, Switzerland, would have a similar effect? It is used as a backdrop for fashion shoots, music videos and advertising in order to create a 'spiritual' atmosphere and at the same time to appeal to a certain target group with architectural knowledge, similar to Disney's use of star architects. Why else would advertising teams undertake the troublesome journey to the Swiss mountains, where the citizens of Vals protect their beautiful village from tourists with a narrow, dangerous street? Clearly the advertising agency believe that the potential buyers of the jeans they shot in front of Zumthor's stone walls would recognise the building. Despite this social and cultural use of his work, or perhaps because of it, Zumthor can continue to live like a lonely monk in the mountains, a lifestyle that reflects a certain self-marketing not unlike that of the shy Helmut Lang.

The recent activities of Rem Koolhaas and Jacques Herzog, two star architects of the second generation, reflect a new shift. No longer interested in the strategy of signature buildings that was employed by the first generation, they are emphasising the firm as more important than the design. In a well-calculated marketing strategy, Koolhaas' Office for Metropolitan Architecture (OMA) and Herzog and de Meuron (HdM) announced the formation of a joint firm for the construction of a new hotel in Manhattan. Even a failure would be secondary to this announcement. Both offices refer to the strategies of the fashion industry, where branding and marketing power are essential. Creative power becomes virtually anonymous within the group, although in the fashion industry importance is attached to the fact that 'creatives', hired per season, should be well known at least to insiders. OMA and HdM believe that through the conjunction of the two brands they will gain access to bigger commissions and markets.

In 'Superfluous Architecture' [1994], I still attributed to architecture in this environment of total commercialisation such roles and qualities as research, experimentation or the acknowledgement of a new realism. Since then, however, it has increasingly become event or entertainment architecture. My question as to whether architecture can withstand the world domination of consumerism has now been answered: every cathedral and museum is a shop. At the moment, it seems that the strategy of OMA and HdM is the only one that can – open-eyed and reflexive – control, question or accelerate this development. The last few years have clearly demonstrated that even refusal leads to consumption. Architecture is 'promotional architecture' or it is not architecture at all. ▵

E-tail

and the Increasing Importance of Retail Innovation

In the last few years, the development of virtual retail space on the Internet has called into question the future viability of physical stores. Here, Julian E Markham, author of *The Future of Shopping* (1998), explains why the development of e-tail has led to an increasing emphasis on shopping environments that use design to surprise and delight their customers and surpass their competitors.

Price alone, as an attraction is unlikely to produce an enjoyable shopping experience. Low prices can be associated with pleasurable shopping, but pleasure also includes convenience perhaps, and more importantly, entertainment. 'Entertainment' can have several meanings. To some, it evokes the experience of shopping in stores that originated in the entertainment industry, such as Disney or Warner Brothers' shops. Others may think of other innovative groups, such as Sharper Image with its display and sale of fascinating, modern design, mainly in the form of electronic gizmos. For most families, it is the simple pleasure of a few hours spent window-shopping, making special purchases, enjoying a meal and a day out. For fashion shoppers, especially at high-branded stores, it is often the feeling of engulfment within an ambience of the brand's personality, or identification with those who endorse it – Ivana Trump or Posh Spice, for example. If such discrimination is evident the need for personal attention so important, it is difficult to see how an impersonal computer screen can be satisfying.

For most retailers, the early 1990s showed the smallest sales gains in 30 years. This decline has provoked a reassessment of retail environment strategies. One of the most important changes is summed up in the term 'value marketing'. There was a powerful tendency to move away from luxury items and towards more practical, less costly alternatives, which are perceived to do the job just as well. The manufacturers at the higher end of the market have all faced significant problems. Mercedes, Saks Fifth Avenue, Ralph Lauren and IBM are examples of this. On the other hand, as exampled in America, companies such as Wal-Mart, Lexus and The Gap, which developed strategies to meet the needs of consumers in the middle range, prospered.

As the move towards consumers' needs, and not only their desires, continues, the most effective means of marketing and distribution changes correspondingly. Sales had originally been stimulated by the 'image and trappings of luxury' through advertising, merchandising and packaging. Now, practices are emphasising value and solid information as the basis on which to make a decision to purchase. The spectacular performance of the world's largest retailer, Wal-Mart, has prompted new formats and strategies of mass merchandising to be followed by almost all sectors of retailing. Yet, there is a blurring of the divide. Mercedes offer their luxury image but a small budget car; Tesco offer low prices with high quality and attractive store design.

Today, it's no longer enough to do it well, you also need to do it new. The realities of today's rapidly changing and extremely competitive markets are challenging all parts of traditional market wisdom and practice. These changes are each having their effect on the strategies of producers through advertising and marketing media and the mechanisms of the retail system itself. The entire economy is being influenced by innovation and the introduction of 'something new' – such as the Internet. Nothing in recent times has so quickly transformed a simple industrial economy into the more complex, rapidly changing intelligent economy that now exists.

A new age of innovation is now in progress. The key words are 'surprise', 'delight', 'surpass'.

The prerequisite for success has moved beyond being a low-cost producer, having TQM (Total Quality Management), customer obsession and JIT (Just-In-Time), procedures which are found in all successful organisations. That is, they are not considered options for success, but essentials. The new factor needed to succeed today is the introduction of true innovation, which not only dramatically impacts on existing operations, but actually surprises and delights customers by surpassing their expectations.

With cost control procedures in place, new, fast-inventory replenishment systems operational and stores at every sales generator, retailers are finding it difficult to find ways to make their offers different from that of these competitors. They are also struggling to increase their thin profit margins. Their objective is to create a total design concept ranging from store layout, to signage, to different products that makes them different from those competitors. They want to promote a message of being distinctive, not more of the same.

Retailers themselves are instituting designs for store formats that recognise customers' demand for more than static shopfronts and displays. These may be used in the proper sense of marketing, to indicate to the shopper what can be seen inside. They should invite and entice the window-shopper to enter a world that is exciting, welcoming and likely to offer satisfaction, both

in terms of personal experience and in terms of the goods on offer. The shop visit should hold out the hope of a fulfilling personal experience and service satisfaction. In such a scenario, it is extremely important that the delivery and perception meet the expectation. This is a dangerous game. For example, the Minimalist 'art gallery' layout - a long parade from entrance to display racks - makes some shoppers feel as if they are in a goldfish bowl. Those shoppers are unlikely to return. The design must meet the first principal objective: enhance the retail offer, assist the sale and make the customer feel good.

Architecture and spatial design have become major elements in retail presentation. Their place in the overall scene and promotion of the retailer, the merchandise and the message is a delicate balance of complementary aesthetics, seduction and comfort. In some cases the architecture overpowers the product and that raises a serious question about whether the attraction should be the store or the merchandise. Should the focal point be the set or the actor? Most retailers and shopping-centre owners will believe that the property is an envelope to contain the merchandise. It should invite you to open it and discover what you want inside, be captivated and want to visit it again and again.

As a result, retail design in some instances invites the consumer to feel actively involved while viewing merchandise. Shoppers are responding by expecting more, with store designs that incorporate innovative and original features. Customers' increasing experience and knowledge, therefore, will drive the way in which

Janson Goldstein, KBond, LA, 2000.
KBond in LA, a menswear shop designed as an ever-evolving art installation, epitomises the present climate of innovation in retail design. It was conceived by James Bond and Karen Kimmel. Bond is a freelance art director and prop stylist who has worked on award-winning music videos and commercials for Madonna, the Rolling Stones, Tricky, PJ Harvey and Nike,

while Karen Kimmel is an installation artist. The concept of KBond meshes together the partners' creative and commercial backgrounds. It is setting out to raise the standards of the modern man's shopping experience. This it aims to do through its departmentalisation of products: sport, classic and new methods – an area that is set to push men into

fresh areas of innovation and invention in their dressing habits. Colour-coded postcards communicate to KBond's customers: green for upcoming events; red for fresh delivery of goods; blue for a sale; and orange for a website update. The KBond graphic indicating this coding is regularly reinterpreted on the store's main wall and simultaneously imprinted on a limited-edition T-shirt.

a store's attractions are implemented. The 'new breed' of consumer is likely to be looking for presentation that is more attention grabbing, and retailers are turning into more than mere stockists of products in the traditional sense. Instead, they are moving to attractive locations that entertain in themselves. The future should see some exciting changes in the showcasing of merchandise for the customer.

Against this background, it is difficult to see how an Internet screen can replace the personal experience of shopping. Sensual stimulants such as feel, smell, taste, are absent in a virtual world. Retailers, with their thousands of real stores, representing billions of pounds and huge stocks, employees and investment, are aware that the Internet is unlikely to be successful without the participation of brand names. However, they also recognise the power of the Net to promote and advertise in a way never seen before, to harness e-commerce, promote and advertise the retail opportunity, provide a catalogue of products for sale in an attractive on-call series of Web pages, supply information on availability and locations, and sell to the browser. Sales are additional to the retail revenue at stores, return of goods may generate additional sales and visits and the advertising is worldwide, cheap and interactive.

The Internet is therefore a valuable retail tool as an ancillary to personal shopping at stores.

Design and delivery of the image in reality should be uplifting; be it the building, aesthetics, merchandise or service. Compare this with shopping on the Net. It is a widely held opinion that few people with time to spare would choose to sit in front of a computer screen for hours, when they could be shopping in person, in a welcoming, efficient, well-stocked and attractive environment. The advantages of the latter include the enjoyment of discovery and selection in one's own time. Rather than at the pace of the Net, immediacy of ownership, seeing a large range of merchandise rather than a small selection, viewing the true colour, trying and handling the product, stimulation through the shop's environment and design, and human contact. We are human beings, not robots and with the help of retail designers the human instinct will continue to enjoy the entertainment provided through personal involvement in shopping. ⚤

Fear and Learning or

Branding and theme-ing are at their most dramatic in Las Vegas. Kevin Rhowbotham, Alphaville, explores the city and the 'continuous programmatic plate' of the casino-hotels.

the Campaign Trail

These fantastical structures have instigated and tested out global homogenisation and many of the current commercial retail trends that are now having such an impact on fashion and architecture.

Notes
1. 'Kis' is an abbreviation of
kilograms.
2. Arlo Guthrie.
3. Directed by Adrian Lyne in
1993.
4. Aspects of a continuous loss
characterise the state of
contemporary capitalism.
Commodity-spend attempts to
recover this loss by means of
an empty signifier. The image
of the commodity promises
much more than it can
possibly supply in terms of
satisfaction or recompense.
5. City populations are
composed increasingly from
both permanent and transitory
populations. The expansion of
tourism in recent decades has
seriously affected the
populations of major cities,
influencing and distorting their
peculiar economies.
Contemporary urban
economics is based in part on
these phenomena.
6. Circus Circus featured
trapeze acts above the heads
of the gamblers at the casino.
7. Bernard Tschumi's
Architecture and Disjunction,
MIT Press (Cambridge, Mass),
1994.
8. The Web has created a
dramatic transformation in the
nature of commerce, for
architecture most especially
and most importantly in the
area of retail. The nature of
urban retail outlets, the way
they are organised and in
which they present
commodities for sale is
undergoing a number of
dramatic transformations. The
appearance of Web retail has
constituted a re-organisation
of traditional divisions within
the global marketplace and
forced their reorganisation.
The most dramatic is the
association of the retail and

Although, within this present period of positivism and superficiality, fashion has been recast as an important aspect of the economy, it still harbours those aspects of the culture of capitalism that made it so reviled by those in the arts who wished for a cultural agenda with a well-defined teleology or end cause. That which is fashionable is necessarily short-lived, and fits itself to the machinations of market capitalism and to those aspects of commodity exchange that determine its duration. What, if anything, can be relevant within fashion to architecture?

The question is an enduring one because there is something within the discipline of architecture, and to a large extent this is increasing, that lends itself to the fleeting and the diaphanous. Currently there is a trend away from formal preoccupations towards an interest in programmatics. A trend that is, I have no doubt, a formalism of sorts, but which has nevertheless refocused the debate upon rudely commercial themes.

If we are to ask then, what is the link between fashion and architecture, it might be something like the current preoccupation with branding and its possible architectural corollary. Citing Vegas is pertinent in this regard because it is the predominant context in which branding has established its most significant architectural moment, and the place in which trends in commercial retail design have been instigated and, in a way, tested. Both branding (the identification of a commodity product and product lines with a discrete set of designed conditions) and theme-ing (the identification of commodity products with a narrative or theme) are dramatically magnified within the Vegas context. Consequently, Vegas provides an ideal vantage from which to reflect upon the relationship of fashion and architecture.

Vegas, Vegas
Flying in from Los Angeles,
Bringin' in a couple of kis,[1]
Don't open my bags if you please
Mr Business man.[2]
What mediates my image of Vegas most powerfully, after the squalid demise of Elvis, is probably Hunter S Thompson's vile reflection *Fear and Loathing in Las Vegas* (1971), a book that charts with surgical precision the magnified spirit of Vegas from the personal perspective of a febrile journalist and addict.

Two aspects of this account strike me as wholly true. Firstly, that the inebriate impression of Thompson's antihero is a narcotic Vegas as a stage of appearances, a documentation or reportage of events, in which the spectacle of commodification is itself the primary object for sale. Secondly, that it offers very little in terms of substance in return. What is on sale is the event, either directly staged, as in the case of Steve Wyn's Disneyfic(a)tion of a book theme at the Hotel Treasure Island, or as a partial dispossession: the loss of money at the gaming tables. In both cases, nothing is returned to the purchaser other than a sense of a thrilling loss that must, in order to be reinstated or re-experienced, be serially repeated. The point of Vegas is not to win a fortune or a night with Demi Moore (as Robert Redford did in the movie *Indecent Proposal*[3]) but to lose in the process of attempting it and by doing so to aggravate a desire to continue. The film illustrates one thing starkly: that conventional values are suspended by an infatuation with loss.[4]

Obsession and magnification are perhaps synonymous with the extra-urban image of Vegas as a place predicated on the glamorisation of the event as supreme commodity. From the time of the Sinatra 'rat pack', the leading establishments such as the Stardust and Caesar's Palace were multiprogrammed buildings housing hotel, auditorium and casino facilities among others. The casino was the primary programme, taking the largest margin of profit, but it was fronted by a major-name show – Frank Sinatra, Debbie Reynolds, Dean Martin, Elvis Presley, Tom Jones, etc. The show acted as a national draw for the casino. It performed as a national event-attractor.

Since the 1950s, the nature of the Vegas casino has changed with the nature of its spending populations. At today's prices, an average visitor in the mid-1950s would expect to spend in the region of $7,000 on a typical trip. Today, the figure is closer to $700, though the annual profit for the casino city has never been larger. Since the 1950s, fundamental changes have occurred in the marketing of the Vegas casino/hotel to meet this change in demographic patterns. The contraction of the amount individuals are prepared to spend has been associated with a change in the types of visitors themselves. The rise of postpermanent populations,[5] of selective tourist economies, marked the nature of the Vegas economy from the first. Since the 1950s, however, the expansion of tourism has made a significant impact on the nature of retailing in major population centres. Vegas has witnessed dramatic transformations in its demographic and sociometric mix of visitors. More families and foreign tourists have ensured that the classic Vegas casino/hotel has moved into new and more adventurous programmatic experiments. Circus Circus[6] extended the classic Vegas programmatic mix. The once detached event – a Cher concert or a Boxing world title fight for example – was now integrated within the gaming plate itself. The event-attractor and the primary programme were now allied for the first time.

Above
The Venetians is a composite
of all the wonders of Venice.

Opposite
The Paris and Bellagio are
two of the more recent
casino-hotels.

leisure industries. The recent
Time, Warner, AOL, EMI
concurrent mergers has seen
the creation of the first global,
retail/entertainment
conglomerate, which has the
facility to provide publishing,
cinema and popular music to
a huge number of Internet
users. At a current market
value of $2,000 billion it has
a capitalisation twice the size
of the UK's current GDP
(Gross Domestic Product). The
purchasing power of such a
capital-rich leviathan and its
interest in pressing home a
global brand image behind its
ubiquitous web presence
makes large sections of the
world's hypercities – Paris,
London, New York, Tokyo –
vulnerable to territorialisation.
Not only is it entirely possible
for such a commercial
phenomenon to territorialise
large areas of the central
districts of these cities, but
the process is already under
way. Nike Town is a branded
neighbourhood, a kind of
forerunner of a comprehensive
branded district in which tens
of blocks of midtown
Manhattan, for example, could
be assimilated and dedicated

It is a traditional trait of the Vegas casino that
the spectacle of gaming is remote and detached
from the mundane city outside. The casino is
a separate place, without windows, internal
divisions, clocks or any other gauge of the outer
city. It is the labyrinth at the centre of the
complex, through which all parties must pass
in order to gain access to the other parts of the
casino/hotel programme. Combining event-
attractor and primary programme was a first
step to the ubiquitous programming of the
gaming floor.

The Coincidence of Architectural
Theory and Vegas

Certain developments at the theoretical limits
of architectural practice have recently come
together. Of primary importance is the wider
acceptance of the ideas of Bernard Tschumi,
most specifically concerning the reappraisal
of an exclusive Modernist programmatics.
Tschumi's investigations into what is widely
referred to as 'cross-programming' – the
juxtaposition of otherwise exclusive and
antithetical programmes, such as sky-diving
in the elevator shaft, or roller skating in the
Laundromat[7] – provoked not only a reinvigorated
interest in the programme per se, but also the
idea that distinct programmes might be
juxtaposed in the same space rather than
exclusively preserved in a cellular arrangement.
The notion of a broad floor-plate that juxtaposed
different programmatic types without separation
now became possible. Speculation concerning an

architecture that might contain this kind of
programmatics has led to a number of developments
that extend the floor slab as a deep-plan facility and
further develop it in section as a continuous ramped
plate unencumbered by fixed vertical circulation.

The interest of practices such as OMA and MRVDV in
this approach stems from a coincidence of these issues
and has developed into a full-blown topological or
landscape paradigm in the work of FOA, Jesse Reiser,
Stanley Allen and more recently Peter Eisenman and
Zaha Hadid. What has driven this shift compositionally
is a wish to rid the floor plate of all intervening objects,
to make of it a space constructed from conditions of
intraprogrammatic flow rather than a space implied
by the navigation of fixed objects or ranked cells. Its
derivation owes a great deal to the nature of the Vegas
casino/hotel and the development of an event/
programme amalgamation. From this perspective,
architectural planning is no longer concerned with the
division of space into discrete and discontinuous entities
like eggs in a basket. Rather, this space, which we
might call 'field space' for the sake of this argument,
has a continuous quality of subtending flows,
thickenings and areas of high density, more like a
weather map than a traditional architectural plan.

Additionally, field space embraces the homogeneity
of globalisation through the figure of the continuous
programmable plate.[8] The Vegas casino is its
quintessential paradigm. All probable programmes
are simultaneously present in one deep space; a field
of ubiquitous programmatic inclusions in which
everything is simultaneously available on the same
surface. The apparent limitlessness of this space, the
lack of internal divisions, the remoteness and invisibility

to the retail of a single conglomerate brand.

9. The predominant compositional paradigm of 20th-century Modernism depends upon the association of abstract objects or figures, placed against and contrasted with a neutral, nonfigured, empty background. This is a play on the presence and absence of graphic objects within the perimeter of the drawing plane or the canvas, a juxtaposition of the configured object constructed in contradistinction to an undifferentiated and receding background; what has come to be known as a figure/ground, or object/field opposition. 'Object' is defined as a form, or collection of forms, that sustains identifiable figuration in contrast to an undifferentiated, formless background. This background, the 'field', surrounds and delimits distinct objects with a continuous and, most importantly, a nonperspectival space. The difference between object and field is one of relative quality and extension. A field remains a field only insofar as it can be clearly discerned as that which is not the object and vice versa. But within the limits of the drawing plane, objects and fields maintain a degree of interchangeability, which is both telescopic and hierarchical, connoting primary, secondary and tertiary (etc) strategraphical levels of complexity. Objects, which have significant extensions within a primary field, constitute secondary fields when smaller objects are superimposed upon them. They act as fields to these smaller groupings in the same way as the drawing plane constitutes an ultimate field within which the most extended objects of the composition are delineated. Clearly, this hierarchical interchange is infinitely extendible.

Kevin Rhowbotham is a founder member of architectural and product design firm Alphaville. He is currently Diploma Unit Master at the Architectural Association, London, and is the author of two books: *Form to Programme* (1995) and *Field Event/Field Space* (1999). He has been Distinguished Visiting Professor at the Department of Architecture, University of Illinois at Chicago, 1998, and Visiting Professor for Architecture and Urbanism at the Technical University, Berlin, 1995–97.

of the perimeter container, reduce any opportunity to fashion architectural effects to the floor and the ceiling. While the ceiling remains the plane of major spectacle, the floor is coded to exaggerate the total spend. In the contemporary Vegas casino/hotel, retail has been comprehensively introduced to the gaming plate. Navigation within the casino floor is now articulated by set-piece retail structures offering not only food and refreshment but also branded goods. Within the gaming plate – organised increasingly on a landscape model – the most desirable branded commodities are distributed as brand islands.

The architectural organisation of these spatialities has now passed beyond a familiar or picturesque Modernist vocabulary. The organisation of the multiprogrammed plate can no longer be achieved by neoplastic or classical compositional devices, which have concentrated traditionally on the organisation of objects within an undifferentiated field of space. The organisation of objects as programmatic containers and dividers is now redundant. What this new architecture requires is the inversion of the traditional object/field relationship, moving away from an object-based architecture to one now dominated by field.[9] The organisational vocabulary of architecture is currently undergoing a dramatic transformation. Having forsaken the articulation of 'objects' in favour of flows, densities, horizons, territories, concentrations, singularities, attractors and so on, a new vocabulary is emerging that deliberately avoids the discontinuities of an objectness and a containing space.

From Vegas to the new leisure/retail plate market-oriented Western governments keen to embrace a 'third way' deregulatory policy have wholly abdicated to the private sector their responsibility for directing urban redevelopment. Although this traditionally rests on commercial-developer control, the creation of new hypermonopolies with unprecedented access to global markets through the Web threatens to shift responsibility away from the commercial developer directly into the hands of brand conglomerates. Competitive attempts to dictate global markets have led to the establishment of major suburban developments in pursuit of substantial brand identification.

Achieving the regeneration of sectors of the hypercity urban core may well be feasible on a grand scale only by these market players. The reason for doing it is to associate the full spectrum of leisure programmes, from participatory sports and low-key entertainments to spectator sports facilities, even some form of public gaming, within a continuous retail plate.

Much has been made of the iconography of some of the more recent Vegas casino/hotels such as New York New York, Paris, the Bellagio, The Mirage, and Treasure Island. Themeing of the object has been taken as the most significant aspect of the architecture of these commodity palaces. Such a view is misleading, however, because it overlooks the more important programmatic transformations that have shaped them. ᐃ

Branding – Signs, Symbols or Something Else?

Charles Jencks in conversation with

Rem Koolhaas

Rem Koolhaas continues to challenge received ideas of what architecture is and how the city works, or doesn't, as the case may be. In this, he is reminiscent of Le Corbusier. His research, though explicitly separated from his design, nevertheless feeds it directly. In this, he is reminiscent of Robert Venturi and Denise Scott-Brown. His fat books, such as *S.M.L.XL* of 1996 and the soon-to-appear *Harvard GSD Guide to Shopping*, are radical explorations of their subject, written with a black-humoured, deadpan wit comparable to that of Andy Warhol. His style and methods of thinking have been cloned successfully both by his students at Harvard and his compatriot architects in Holland. In this respect he is like Palladio, a ventriloquist. With his work and writing he has continued to lead and change architecture, sometimes like a prophet, at times like the Pied Piper. Charles Jencks cross-examines him about his work for Prada and his thoughts on branding.

CJ First of all, I can see that you're very interested in global culture now. It's something that I've been calling 'globcult' for many years, because it's run by the multinationals – 380 multinationals control 80 per cent of the global market – and they produce a culture that is really glob rather than global, but I think you look on it very positively, don't you?

RK It's not that I look at it positively per se, but you have to look at it in a nuanced way. You can discern certain aspects that enable a positive alignment. It's not that I embrace global culture uncritically. On the contrary, our allergies are probably to a large extent the same ones. But I think, for instance, if you talk about Prada, that is an enterprise that has a global reach and is involved in a global strategy, but it's also clear that it's not 'glob' in your terms.

CJ I realise that when you talk about shopping as 'the terminal human condition' you are critical; you see the nuanced side. I'm not saying that you don't see that side, but basically when you brand yourself 'OMA' and then 'AMO', and you use that other branding, 'Yen + Euro + US Dollar = Yes', you're saying 'yes' to globcult in a way that others aren't. That's all I'm saying, but you do see its downside ...

RK I think that as an architect it would be disingenuous to do anything else. Architects are dependent on commissions, and it is very clear that in that overall regime of 'Yes' there are a number of theoretical commissions. Some of them are mediocre, some of them are evil and some of them are positive. We are determined to retain those distinctions and not work for what is evil, to work as little as possible for what is mediocre and to work as much as possible for what is positive.

CJ In fact, though, you do talk about 'junk space' with a certain disdain, a certain annoyance and a certain kind of resigned – if not cynicism, then despair. I wonder ... 'junk space' is a kind of trademark of yours, is it?

RK Like everything we do, you have to see it in context. I was really stunned by the fact that certain formal aspects of the current spatial condition had never been taken seriously as such. They were always explained as symptoms, but they were never really investigated for their own sake. So what I did was simply look at that spatial condition, which in my view is a

completely unique and unprecedented one, and which is really triggered by the endlessness of buildings, that is in itself given by air-conditioning, the escalator and by the current 'Yes' regime. I simply looked at what the implications are. There's no disdain in the whole thing. It's more like an almost scientific inventory of its qualities.

CJ But you know as well as I do that after Robert Venturi wrote *Learning from Las Vegas* and he and Denise Scott-Brown said they weren't being judgmental about it, very soon description, science and value-free urbanism turned into prescription, high-fliers and what you should do. It seems to me that you're the first one since the Venturis to look in depth at what I would call 'inflation space', and you're aware of its downside. But do you not think that, as with the Venturis, description turns by alchemy into prescription? You may not want it to, but from writing about shopping, you're now designing for shopping, so you're turning what was analysis and research into prescription.

RK Why is this prescription?

CJ Because, just as the Venturis promoted signs not symbols, as far as I was concerned, and high-fliers ...

RK The Venturis looked at the phenomena very seriously and then extracted from those phenomena a new syntax that they actually began to apply in their own work. I don't think I'm doing the same thing at all, although I totally admire what they did so I'm not trying to disassociate myself in terms of being better in that sense. But there's really nothing prescriptive in the entire shopping book at all. It's a series of interpretative and analytical cartographies and, of course, what it has meant is that I now understand the phenomenon of shopping much better. If I'm doing shops, there is no dogmatic influence from the reseach, and our work continues to be a sequence of very specific and ungeneralisable propositions.

CJ That sounds to me like Ebenezer Howard saying, 'This is just a diagram, not a prescription'. Fair enough. I understand what you're saying. When you talk about 'MOMA Inc' – the Museum of Modern Art Incorporated – you critique the way they've blurred the zone between culture and shopping. There's a seamless logic in the way the museum turns culture into a form of retail. Isn't that right?

RK No, I think it's different. What I tried to trigger through 'MOMA Inc' is the idea that museums right now may still pretend that they're temples of culture, but we all know they have completely different agendas

Opposite left
Portrait of Rem Koolhaas by Sanne Pepper.

Opposite right
Koolhaas's 'Yen + Euro + US Dollar = Yes'. Graphic produced for research on Schipol Airport, The Netherlands.

and that the sheer volume of people they have to process in a single day has simply tilted the balance or mutated the concept. They can no longer be places of contemplation or of complete authenticity in terms of a conversation between a work of art and a person. The numbers of visitors alone, and increasingly the role culture plays in the global economy, don't support that fiction. Our project was intended more to declare the end of a particular fiction. It's not a reproach that they blur the issue; it's more a comment that without the recognition of this new condition we're all forced to blur and be confused by what is what.

CJ Wouldn't you say that the problem also of Tate Modern, with the biggest shop for art books in the world, is again a kind of seamless continuity between the shop and the other role of art – the more autonomous role of appreciation. Both the Museum of Modern Art and Tate Modern, under the logic of shopping, blur that distinction. In other words, couldn't you be more critical than you're now being?

RK Basically, what we tried to do in MOMA is say, 'given this situation, you can then articulate it in the design'. Then you can imagine a museum that is consumed at two speeds, or three speeds, or four speeds, or a museum that has a commercial circuit and a noncommercial circuit, or one that has one shift that is purely superficial and another that is in-depth. What we are trying to say is if that's the situation, it then opens up a completely new zone of danger and a completely new zone of potential. If the Tate is an example of anything, it's that by not explicitly acknowledging a new situation it continues a tenuous relationship between the two.

CJ Then we agree. The architecture should make clear that the marriage has happened but that they're two different things. Culture isn't the same as shopping.

RK No.

CJ And both of these museums blur the distinction. Anyway, I want to look at branding for a minute. It's gone on, obviously, since the Middle Ages, when families and cities were branded. In our era it was Coca-Cola who perhaps got the biggest brand in the 1910s. In architecture since the 1950s, IBM has been totally branded by Paul 'brand' Rand and has opened up the recent history, which you discuss in your book, *Harvard GSD Guide to Shopping*, particularly focusing on the Nike 'swoosh'. What do you have to say about that history of the development of the brand towards a kind of symbol, like a heraldic or national symbol?

RK I think that there are two kinds of identity. The current trend of branding is towards a terminal identity. It narrows the identity to one immutable and invariable condition. That is a very conservative and reactionary form of branding, which in a way has as its main mission to exclude surprise and therefore to attract anyone who wants only one known thing in the largest possible numbers. I think there's much more interesting work that you can do with a brand or any identity, which is to make it more variable and less redundant in terms of its significance. If I'm not mistaken – and I may be very mistaken – what is developing is an American ideology of the brand, which is the death knell of further development and therefore ultimate reactionary stability, and a European idea of the brand as something that is alive and that can assume many different identities and incur further development. When Prada briefed us, their key words were 'unpredictability' and 'variability'. If you look at Disney, there it's a permanent return to the 'original', not-too-dangerous condition.

CJ But you have to admit, say, the importance of blank architecture, or Minimalism, as a background for the brand. It's quite obviously the case that since the late 1980s, with the Minimalist movement of Armani, Yves St Laurent, Jigsaw and Issey Miyake, and architects like the Pawsons and Silvestrins, the culture of shopping has turned Modernism and Minimalism into the perfect background for the brand. In other words, the seamless fit …

RK I totally agree.

CJ So a brain-dead Minimalism in the late stages of Modernism has given up the old alibi of spirituality and fallen into …

RK One thing that I find interesting is that only now, in this situation, is the issue of the 'quality' of the architectural detail becoming crucial. Detail as the smoothest possible transition is the final sellout of Minimalism to the cult of consumption. That is why we always were, and still are, interested in resistance on the level of detail and choice of materials.

CJ You work for Prada. You've said that in the two last years, Prada has opened 200 stores and has really achieved global saturation.

RK 'Saturation' is not the idea – rather, global distribution.

CJ Global distribution. So you're looking for new strategies, and you've come up with new strategies. One of them is a kind of ironic inversion of MOMA, because instead of turning culture into shopping, you're turning shopping into culture, as I understand it, in SoHo, New York. You have display areas on tracks that can be pulled around into clusters so that you can uncluster them and then recluster them.

RK You can unleash this display system as shopping, or contract it as culture.

CJ When you pull the tracks together, you open up a place for an auditorium. Is that right?

RK Yes. Then almost the entire store becomes a cultural space.

CJ And the reason for that is to counter the way in which shops and boutiques have taken over the whole of SoHo? It's to resist that, is it?

RK It's basically to begin to re-enrich the area, since shopping is now so pervasive there. The one experience it doesn't offer is that of the public and the strictly noncommercial realms. I think it's interesting to try to introduce them.

CJ I'm sure you're right. Having been into Donna Karan on Bond Street, and those kinds of shops, there's a trend in the way that the art exhibition and the choosing of clothes are both the choosing of identity. The choosing of a personal physical identity and the choosing of art meet each other at this point. In a way, you're taking this trend to its ultimate conclusion. You catch the wave, watch it break beneath you and push out your surfboard in front. You also use sexuality in the stores. You devise ways of changing in public and private so that you can see yourself from behind, and I suppose other people can watch you. You use suggestive veiling and all these devices that are already in the shop, and you push them to the next step. Do you think that's true?

RK Yes, but I don't think it's necessarily connected to sexuality. It's more that we extend the ways in which you can judge fit. It's more about the self. Perhaps because clothes now assume larger responsibility for the whole identity, it's more important than previously

not only to look at the fit in the specific sense but also at the impression it makes. It's extending the repertoire of judgement. All of that is private except that if you want to show it to somebody else, you can show it indirectly. You're never looked over by others. The point is that you could send an image as an e-mail to a partner who's on the other side of the world.

CJ So you facilitate dressing for other people as well as for yourself. Another tactic you use in San Francisco is what you call a kind of super foam-*poché*. Then you excavate into it. You connect this, as I understand it, with a kind of ultimate new junk space, which is made out of Sheetrock and other existing elements. Could you explain what you have in mind there?

RK It's more to do with the fact that perhaps an important aspect of junk space is the increasing insubstantiality of all the materials. I mean, entire buildings are now made of Sheetrock, as you know. That again is one of those revolutions in architecture that has never been articulated by anyone – except perhaps by the Venturis. But there is no architect, that I know, who is making this an issue. There are many spaces in architecture now that are neither solid, nor void, nor in between. So it was an attempt to investigate whether, given the fact that everything is becoming more insubstantial and given the fact that in many plans or architectural conditions you have a tendency to put some filler in, we might develop the filler as an architectural condition. That is, design, or invent, a kind of foam.

CJ Your foam-*poché* is solid, void and air – all three together. I think you're right to connect it up with the Venturis, but one of the problems with the Venturis and their looking at an environment where signs dominate, is that they have less of a commitment to, let's say, architectural construction and the traditional architectural values of building. On the one hand the kind of thing that Frampton would criticise them for, and on the other, the kind of thing I would criticise them for: not understanding the distinction between a sign and a symbol. In other words, they tend to use signs stuck on backgrounds or ornaments stuck on building boards. These become insubstantial selling points, as Le Corbusier said, like the ostrich feather stuck in a hat rather than something profoundly related to the hair. Would you comment on the failure of the Venturis to produce a really substantial architecture of signs?

RK I do not want to comment on that, first of all because you're putting words in my mouth, and secondly because, like every architect, they have different kinds of work. But I don't think it's a failure at all. I think that their work is currently incredibly

underestimated. Some of their later works can easily be read as self-critical works in which they address those issues.

CJ I actually think you're right about the importance of the Venturis, but I'm trying to provoke you into ...

RK I don't want to say anything against the Venturis, they are really the last people I want ...

CJ I'm not asking you for that, but rather a comment on signolic architecture, the architecture of signage stuck on buildings.

RK As you know very well, we have never been as affected by the whole semantic issue, and in a way we've preferred to ignore it or only engage with it when it suited us.

CJ You're absolutely right, both about yourself and your relation to the Venturis. I don't want to put words in your mouth, but I do think that in learning from the Venturis one also has to learn from their misunderstanding of what a symbol is.

RK For me, it wasn't necessarily a misunderstanding by the Venturis, but more a misunderstanding in general of the value of symbolism and semantics in architecture. It was part of a larger project, in which you also played a major role, and I think you can now see that some of the applications of that project as a theory were overly literal.

CJ Yes, we agree on that, but it seems to me that in the end architecture is a symbolic art, and it has to tie together function, society, art, light, space and so forth. Symbols make relationships between things, signs are gratuitous stick-ons.

RK But we were always optimistic that symbols would emerge on their own, not by design but by default.

CJ Yes, I agree, in some cases symbols can emerge, especially if the parts coalesce.

Lastly, your Schipol Airport is a kind of orgy of globcult signage, which amazed me – all the possible trademarks and brand images you can get in one explosion. What is the status of Schipol, is it a live project?

RK Actually, you have to separate the presentation from the project. The proliferation of logos was an image to convey to the Dutch government that there were many opportunities for private-public partnerships. It was not an image of the project. The Dutch parliament has just voted to allocate $25 million for further study.

CJ Well, I hope it can pay for all the copyright-breaking you may be doing! You told me that they're more than happy that, under certain circumstances, their trademark and brand can be rebranded. Is that right?

RK It's a typical political situation. Further study is, of course, not a decision to do it and not a decision not to do it, so presumably it's a compromise. Depending on how it's done and depending on how eloquent the sustained impossibility of Schipol becomes in terms of public consciousness, I think it could go either way.

CJ Does the same thing go for the Harvard trademark in the *Harvard GSD Guide to Shopping*? Is that a brand you can use or are they resisting that.

RK The official title is the *Harvard GSD Guide to Shopping*.

CJ I see. A clever way around the copyright and brand problem.

RK Yes.

CJ I should have mentioned that in your book on shopping you quote Joseph Weischar – 'design for effective selling space' – who points out why the area you're investigating produces signs rather than symbols. He says it's based on studying people's behaviour in the shopping zone and gauging their repetitive actions, because 'their minds move along repetitive patterns'. Well, moving along repetitive patterns produces signs not symbols, and the hope that you can turn the tissue of signs and the landscape of signs into something more.

RK I think that shopping/entertainment/infrastructure/ streetshape experience is now so pervasive that the distinctions you mention have collapsed in a new ur-soup that will yield its own rules, categories, methods. I don't feel the time is ripe for syntax, but I guess I never did.

CJ OK, Rem, thank you. No doubt your new book and building for Prada will give some more of the answers. Δ

Opposite
Models for Prada in San Francisco, with its super-foam *poché*.

Beauty is the Beast

An Interview with Jan Kaplicky of Future Systems

Last year, Future Systems' entrance tunnel for Comme des Garçons in New York captured the attention both of the public and the fashion world. Helen Castle of Δ went to interview Jan Kaplicky to find out more about his and his partner Amanda Levete's inspired approach to fashion. The office's two major new projects include a Selfridges department store for Birmingham, and a string of international shops for the Milanese fashion retailer, Marni.

Opposite left
Amanda Levete and Jan
Kaplicky of Future Systems
with their son.

Left
Future Systems' entrance
tunnel to Comme des
Garçons in West Chelsea,
New York.

It is surprising to hear Jan Kaplicky talk about beauty – beauty as an architectural aspiration in itself, rather than as a by-product of design. Though Future Systems' projects are undeniably beautiful – organic forms with the smoothness and plasticity of the aerodynamic – the office is better known for its pioneering attitude towards technology. In the catalogue for the 1998 Future Systems retrospective at the ICA, London, Martin Pawley defined the office's work as an 'advanced technology architecture', a natural successor to the now outmoded High Tech. Since the completion of the NatWest Media Centre at Lord's in 1999, the interest in the technical aspect of Future System's work has spiralled, further fuelled by the excitement generated by the centre's aluminium shell. Semimonocoque, the structure is highly innovative not only in terms of its design but also its manufacture. Prefabricated by a firm of shipbuilders in Cornwall, it was computer dimensioned and cut. This preoccupation with aluminium forms and futuristic imagery was followed through into the office's most high-profile fashion retail project – the entrance tunnel for the Comme des Garçons store in New York. Highly polished and silver coloured, the tunnel creates a space-age transition from a grimy West Chelsea street into the synthetic and fantastically glamorous world of the fashion boutique. A true monocoque structure, without ribs or supports, it was made by Pendennis, the same Falmouth boatyard that produced the media centre.

Since the Winter of 1999, when Future Systems completed Comme des Garçons' New York shop, and finished designing both a curved wall for the Tokyo flagship store and a glass elevation for the shop in Paris, the practice has been overwhelmed with offers of work from fashion houses. This is in spite of the fact that Comme des Garçons' founder, Rei Kawakubo, has been widely publicised as the sole director, if not author, of these projects. Despite being niggled by this matter of attribution, Jan Kaplicky still acknowledges Kawakubo's decision to change the direction of Comme des Garçons' store designs as a defining moment for architecture and fashion. It had got to the point where every shop was about the same thing, whether it was in Bond Street or Madison Avenue. Adjacent stores were all replicating a similar bastardised version of Minimalism. Comme des Garçons was confident and creative enough to opt out of this all-too-pervasive trend. Kaplicky regards this as a turning point in retail design akin to Norman Foster's 1979 shop for

Joseph in Sloane Street, a seminal design that was the result of Joseph Ettedgui's request that Foster do something like Pierre Chareau's Maison de Verre for him. Equally revolutionary were the later Joseph shops, designed by Eva Jiricna in the 1980s, with their intricately constructed steel-truss staircases. These directly addressed the problem of how merchandise should be promoted. By selling clothes in the most attractive way possible, they related what they were selling to those who were buying it. To be able to move forward, there has to be an essential understanding between the client and the architect. Hitting the jackpot hangs on both how brave you are and how brave the client is. A shop has to be sufficiently arty to make an impact. In Future Systems' work, Kaplicky guards against reiteration. He is adamant that over the next few years the office will not take on any more than three, maybe four, new retail clients. In this way, they will be assured of delivering a fresh architectural solution every time, rather than a conveyor belt of shopfits.

Unlike many other architects, Kaplicky and Amanda Levete do not hold fashion at arm's length. Kaplicky believes that architects have much to glean from the fashion world, especially the culture of magazines such as *Vogue* with their adept styling. Magazine styling has an element of fashion that is conspicuously absent in architecture. Notoriously conservative, architects are wary of anything that smacks of the frivolous. This leads not only to a disregard of colour, but also to an all-too-ready acceptance of the ugly. In contrast, the fashion industry is intent on beauty. It revolves around the beauty of the model and the clothes she is wearing.

Kaplicky is unreserved about the fact that he and Levete are setting out to both privilege and create the beautiful in two major new fashion projects – the department store for Selfridges in Birmingham and a series of shops for the Milan-based company Marni. In Birmingham, he wants Future System's main achievement to be aesthetic rather than technical. If it is beautiful everything else will follow. Quite rightly, his stress on the building's appearance reflects Selfridges' importance as a landmark scheme. Selfridges' combined presence, both as a highly sophisticated store and as a piece of innovative architecture, has the potential to inject a new type of cosmopolitan culture

Above
Norman Foster's shop for Joseph in Knightsbridge in 1979, which Kaplicky regards as an important turning point in retail.

Opposite top left
Site model of Future Systems' design for Selfridges' department store in Birmingham. The building's curvaceous form clings to the corner of the site. On top of the store can be seen the trees on the rooftop restaurant.

Opposite top right
Jan Kaplicky's original conceptual sketches for Selfridges in Birmingham, showing its distinctive form and the rooftop restaurant. The store is due for completion in September 2003.

Opposite bottom
Located on the Bullring, the store is specially designed with shop windows that can be viewed by passing vehicles. Photomontage: Hayes Davidson.

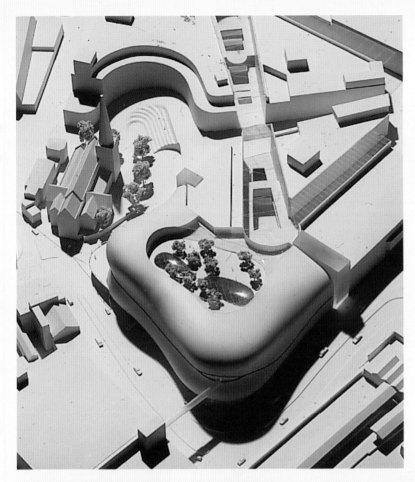

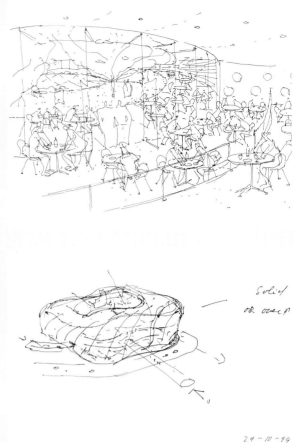

29-10-99

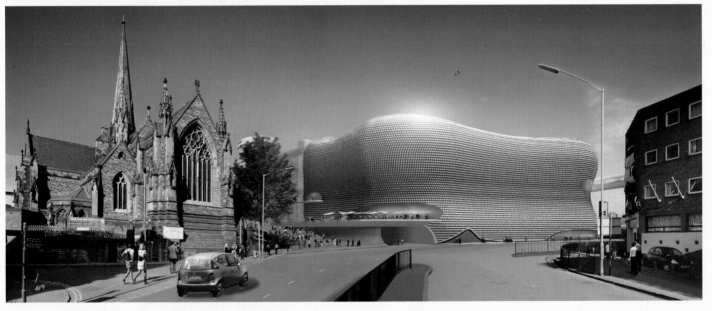

into the city. The store will house six new restaurants as well as a huge variety of luxury goods previously unavailable in the Midlands, or anywhere else outside London. Its sophistication is epitomised by the rooftop garden restaurant, which will be open in the evenings as well as during shop hours. Located on the Bullring in the Digbeth area of the city, Selfridges is part of a larger shopping-mall development. Positioned at one end of the precinct it will anchor the scheme, with a more conventional-style department store at the other. Selfridges, however, bears little relationship to the rest of the mall, which adopts American Po-Mo – the

received style of such speculative developments. In fact, to indicate its separation from the rest of the complex, a wire mesh will be stretched over at the point where the two meet. Looking beyond the shopping centre, Selfridges responds to its corner site, sandwiched between Moor Street and Park Street, and an adjacent 19th-century church. Its soft, curvaceous form clings to its roadside edges and creates a gentle backdrop to the church. The result is a design in which Selfridges have already expressed their supreme confidence. Vittorio Radice has agreed with Future Systems' request to forgo any signage on the outside of the store. For it is evident that such a building, with its extraordinary profile and tiled skin, will need no signing.

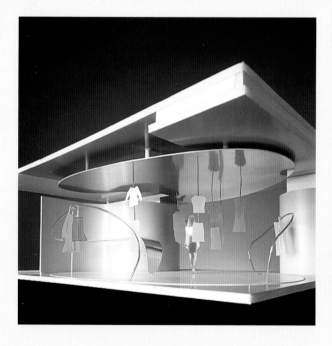

Top left
Clothes rail in the the recently completed
Marni shop in Sloane Street, London.
The rail continues around the interior
and circumscribes the shop floor – a white
terracotta island.

Top right
Clothes hanging from 'trees' in the interior
of Marni, Sloane Street.

Above
Model shot of the Marni shop designed as a
concession in a Tokyo department store.

Right
Model of cladding system being developed
for Selfridges.

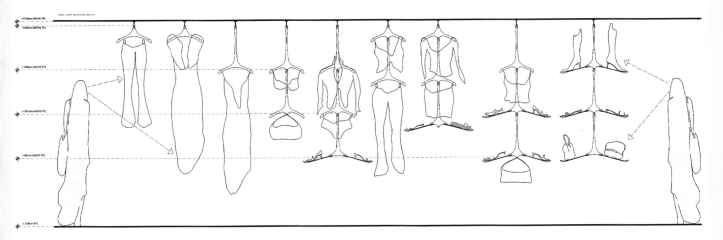

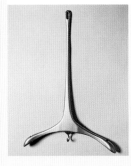

If at Birmingham Future Systems are responding to the changing needs of the city and its aesthetic and cultural vacuum, in their three new shops – London, Tokyo and Milan – for a previously mail-order-based business, Marni, they are accommodating the changing needs of fashion in a totally unprecedented way. Beyond the stainless-steel shield membrane of the front of the Sloane Street store – a mere 1.3 mm thick – will be a long, deep, narrow retail space. The focus of this will be the clothes themselves, hung from long hangers on steel 'trees', which are cantilevered from the floor. In Tokyo where the shop constitutes a concession in a department store, the limited height in the space available has meant that the hangers have had to be suspended directly from the ceiling. Only a small selection of the store's merchandise will be chosen, as items that distil the spirit of a particular season's collection. The design of the shop will give the fashion house further opportunities to express the mood of any one collection by giving them the freedom to alter at will the colour of the resin paint that covers the walls and the floor at the point where the two meet. The main floor area is an island of reconstituted white glass that floats free of the coloured backdrop. With little or no furniture, bar the hangers and their trees - the cash desk is formed out of a steel rail that circles the space – the attention is kept on the clothes. Hanging in the middle of the space, single garments can be walked around, encouraging customers to touch them and experience them as individual sensuous objects.

There is little doubt that Future Systems' design concept for the Marni shops will, as with the Comme des Garçons aluminium entrance in

New York and the curved wall in Tokyo, revolutionise retail design. Instead of imposing rigid architectural spaces, it will make architects think about ways of building stores for designers that are able to move with their collections and place emphasis on the beauty of the clothes themselves. It is in a sense the reverse of the Minimalist trend that employs the luxury of permanent materials – marble, stone and wood – for what add up to no more than disposable interior spaces. More than anything, however, Kaplicky's approach amounts to an appreciation and celebration of that fickle and beautiful thing called fashion. ∆

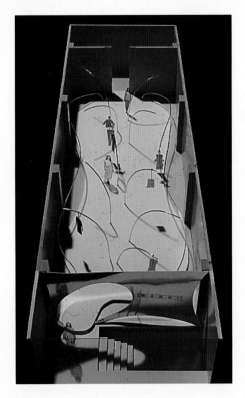

Above top
The range of hangers that Future Systems have developed to display garments in the Marni shops.

Above middle
Prototype of the long hanger developed for the Marni shops.

Right
Model of the Marni shop in Sloane Street, London.

An Interview with David Chipperfield

All Shopped Out

Architect David Chipperfield doesn't believe that there are many more significant ideas to pursue in fashion retail. Art spaces and museums are fast becoming the new shops, as exemplified by the Fondazione Prada in Milan. Shops have had their moment. What, then, attracted him to creating a whole string of stores for Dolce & Gabbana? Why *their* beautiful collections? In an interview with Helen Castle of Δ, Chipperfield told her exactly how architecture should be putting the spotlight back on the clothes.

Dolce & Gabbana's Old Bond Street store by David Chipperfield is in an area of London in which international jewellers predominate, and couturiers take over from ready-to-wear. The interior's basalt floors and crisp white walls render every garment a jewel, shimmering against its dark backdrop. Finely decorated and highly ornate pieces are presented on Chipperfield-designed stands and short, teak rails. Gold-encrusted glittering shoes, handbags, bustiers and coats thus take centre stage. These are matched in richness and intensity only by a range of camp, stand-alone props – gilt Baroque thrones, enormous cacti, zebra-skin rugs and antique mirrors – sourced and supplied by Dolce & Gabbana's merchandising department. Chipperfield's architecture of dark restraint, which places itself at the service of the decorated and ornate, contrasts with the spare spaces that are de rigeur further up the road in New Bond Street. There, the neutral suits hang in packed rails against a light background of expensive, if thinly applied, marbles and limestones. Here, the charcoal basalt is cut as thick as it can be. It steps up to form benches to display accessories and steps down to create a staircase that takes you into the lower floor of the shop. A porous volcanic rock, basalt marks a departure from the now received language of pared-down retail – wood, limestone and cement.

All photos
David Chipperfield Architects,
6-8 Old Bond Street, London.

Though the architecture for the Old Bond Street shop is perfectly adapted to its context and location, it adopts the universal palette of materials that David Chipperfield Architects have developed for Dolce & Gabbana's international chain of shops. The prototype was developed for the Via della Spiga in Milan, followed up by the first London shop and one in Osaka. Stores in London's Sloane Street and Los Angeles have opened with stores in Paris, Madison Avenue in New York, Moscow and Zurich in the pipeline. Each store is created in close dialogue with the fashion designers. The project architect, Andy Groarke shows me the large models that they make and furnish with miniature doll's house versions of Dolce & Gabbana's selected fittings – a tiny chair and zebra rug. The whole process resembles set design, with a similar accent on lighting and the placement of props.

What is clear from talking to David Chipperfield is that the work for Dolce & Gabbana is the result of a very special relationship. When the partners first approached him over two years ago, he was not initially interested in designing more fashion retail space, but he was very impressed with their collection. The most interesting aspect of this kind of design is displaying clothes. Though they cannot be fully appreciated on a hanger, on a beautiful woman or mannequin they look very special indeed. The fineness and decorative quality of the Dolce & Gabbana pieces convinced him that he would like to take on the commission. This was reinforced by the fact that Dolce & Gabbana remain one of the last independent voices in fashion. Their stores are

lively and exciting places to visit. They are one of the few houses to have resisted corporate ownership, and are thus not subjected to the thinning-down effect of marketing and PR departments.

Chipperfield has few illusions as far as the fashion business is concerned: like a vampire, it is prepared to suck you dry and move on. Over the last few years, this effect has been intensified by the corporate stranglehold of a handful of companies over the global fashion market. Retailers desire to be an exact 6 inches in front of their rivals – no more and no less. To sell clothes they need to produce an image, but they can't afford to produce an image at the expense of their clothes. It becomes a process of continually weighing up risk against creativity. For Chipperfield, retail is no longer the architectural playground that it was in the late 1980s. In 1988, as a young, largely unknown architect he designed Issey Miyake's shop in London. It gave him the chance both to launch himself and to develop an architectural language that he had little opportunity to apply elsewhere. Now, however, the architectural style has been set, and retail offers up few architectural challenges. Retailers understand that they sell more clothes in light, open spaces. Chipperfield uses the example of Katherine Hamnett in Sloane Street to illustrate his point. After he designed Equipment next door to Hamnett's shop, Hamnett wanted the same treatment for her baroque, over-the-top Nigel-Coates-designed store. Though Coates' fish tank in the window attracted a great deal of attention, what she needed most was to show her clothes properly.

Chipperfield acknowledges that perhaps there are still innovations to be made. He cites Future Systems' curvy entrance to Comme de Garçons as an example of this and Rem Koolhaas's designs for Prada. But in London and elsewhere, planning restrictions often prohibit a free hand with the facade. The artificial economy of shop design, however, seems to suggest that emphasis will be moving away from architect-designed spaces. It is not what Chipperfield refers to as an 'oranges economy'. Gucci, Christian Dior, Calvin Klein and the like do not expect to recover directly on clothes sales the money they spend on each refit. Most of their revenue comes from perfume. The shops are regarded as promotion, paid for out of the advertising budget. As the language of shop design has become more standardised and more closely controlled by corporate organisations, there is less and less room for innovation and less interest in employing architects. Fashion moving on to other promotional projects. So where does Chipperfield believe the future for fashion and architecture is? In the construction of museums and galleries, as fashion houses like Prada heighten their profile through sponsoring art. ⚙

The Facilitator

An Interview with Rasshied Din

Rasshied Din of Din Associates is an interior designer who has made his name in retail. Din Associates has worked with French Connection for over 12 years and has recently designed London stores for Nicole Farhi, as well as the cosmetics department for Fenwicks in Bond Street. In his book *New Retail*, Din suggests that designers must provide more than style and spatial solutions. They need to be facilitators who help retailers to sell, relaunch and reposition products. In an interview with Helen Castle of *Architectural Design*, he explained just how essential an understanding of brand values has become to fashion retail design.

There are essential tensions at the core of
fashion retail. While entry into mass markets
requires globalisation and standardisation,
fashion is driven from one season to the next by
novelty and innovation. Though it is sustained
by stylists and assimilators, it is driven by
visionary creative people – fashion house and
retailer figureheads. In *New Retail* Rasshied Din
embraces these seemingly conflicting forces.
The big corporate retailers such as Nike Town
and Tesco are given as much space as the
exclusive inspirational stores like Comme des
Garçons, Corso Como 10 and Egg. His practice,
Din Associates, also seems to straddle these
very separate spheres. While in 1997 it designed
the Nicole Farhi shop in Sloane Street, London,
as the launch pad of Farhi Home collection, it is
now developing a concept for the British chain
of stores, Monsoon, which will take on to the
high street the trend for fashion homeware set
by Donna Karan, Rocha, Ralph Lauren and Calvin
Klein. Din's diversity and particular appetite for
the eclecticism of fashion retail can be explained
by his broad definition of a retail designer. He
believes that in order to be successful in today's
global markets, retail designers need to concern
themselves with the broader job of positioning
brands and products rather than limiting
themselves to the look and organisation of
individual shop-floors. It is a multifaceted
approach that, in terms of design, often takes
in advertising, graphics and packaging as well
as interior design.

Din has followed anything but a direct route to his
specialisation in retail. Having worked as an interior
designer in Italy and the UK, he wanted to work in a
multidisciplinary practice. However, only after gaining
further experience in commerce through working in
banks and offices did he start taking up leads for retail-
design jobs. Many of his friends are fashion designers,
so this was something that he took to naturally,
enjoying the speed, the people and the scope for
creativity that fashion offered up. He gained his initial
work for both Next and French Connection through
these contacts in fashion retail. Now, 13 years on,
Din is still working for French Connection, and Din
Associates is designing its third generation of French
Connection stores. This type of long-term partnership
is almost unheard of in the notoriously fickle business
of fashion, which switches designers with every
fluctuation in style. However, what Din has done for
French Connection is to create a corporate look in
which no store is totally alike. This has accommodated
shifting trends, while maintaining underlying
consistency in the company's brand values. Not only
involved in designing the physical space of the stores,
Din Associates has also been responsible for their
graphics. After a number of years directly overseeing
them, it has more recently helped French Connection
to set up its own in-house graphics team.

Given Din's preference for a multidisciplinary
approach, which places the design of retail space in the
broader context of branding and international markets,
how does he view architects' forays into his field? There
are individual trained architects working in teams in his
office – as elsewhere in retail design – but what about

the more conspicuous examples: the named architects whose work has become synonymous with particular fashion houses? Not surprisingly, Din regards this phenomenon from the retailers' point of view. Architects are generally chosen by retailers because they epitomise a certain look or style or a definind moment in time. Conspicuous examples are Nigel Coates for Jigsaw in the late 1980s and John Pawson in the mid 1990s for Calvin Klein. Whereas Coates approach was a narrative baroque – he introduced an aeroplane into the facade of the Knightsbridge branch of Jigsaw – Pawson's was minimal and pared down. On walking down Sloane Street, for instance, in the early to mid-1990s, the shopper could experience very different architectural styles: the precision of Eva Jiricna's interpretation of High Tech in Joseph, Coates' eccentric creation for Katherine Hamnett and David Chipperfield's spare but beautiful Equipment. The consumer was later confused when Joseph and Katherine Hamnett also adopted interiors by Chipperfield, creating a run of shops with little or no differentiation. The overwhelming popularity of white walls and pared-down spaces, however, has led the look of stores to converge. Given that many of the products in high-fashion shops are often very similar, following a season's trend, shops risk losing their point of difference, and thus their identity, among their competitors.

For the high-fashion market, retailers are almost entirely dependent on the edge or point of difference for their key brand value. It is this alone that distinguishes them from, and puts them ultimately ahead of, their competitors. In a simple but acute observation in *New Retail*, Din explains why brands have such a hold over the industry. The old image of luxury goods and glamour – furs, diamonds and expensive cars – no longer exists. Once, quality could be conveyed almost entirely through inherent materials and the skill of manufacturers and craftsmen. Certain countries became synonymous with quality. Italy was regarded, for instance, as the producer of the best leather goods and tailoring. This level of craftsmanship, however, can now be matched by the Third World, which has access to equipment that can replicate the skills involved in making handmade goods. Without the sort of premium that fashion houses once had in a category of luxury materials and the skills that accompanied them, they are totally reliant on their brand. When everyone is following the same global fashions, it is the brand values alone that are relied upon to distinguish one product range from another. Far less tangible than the material qualities of traditional luxury goods, they emanate from the individuals who head the fashion houses. Gurus such as Tom Ford at Gucci, Donatella Versace or Miuccia Prada are responsible for endowing their fashion houses with coherent visions. Fashion houses have to have a clear idea of what they are, if they wish to communicate to their customers a fixed idea of what they are buying into.

One of the greatest threats to this brittle business, built on image and personality, currently lies in globalisation. It is increasingly necessary for fashion houses to be big, if they are to survive and compete with multinational companies such as LVMH. As individual houses become absorbed – YSL by Gucci and Jil Sander

Opposite
Din Associates' flagship store
for Nicole Farhi in Sloane
Street, London, 1998. This
was the launch pad of the new
Farhi Home concept, from
which Farhi started selling
homeware for the first time.
The home products are located
on the first floor in
a gallery-like space; women's
wear is on the ground floor;
and menswear has a clubby
area in the basement.

Above
Fenwicks cosmetics
department, Bond Street,
London, 2000.

by Prada – there is also the possible danger that original brands could lose their way and become obscured. The challenge lies in successfully incorporating unique brands, which encourage rather than smother distinctness and individuality, into conglomerates. Though many of the companies are feeling the pull to expand or absorb, the size of a fashion house or a corporate group can also make it unwieldy, disabling it from responding fast enough to trends and market forces. Even once it realises world dominance, there is the danger that it has become too pervasive. Highly visible and present at every airport, and even in local chain stores, it can lose its exclusivity – the very thing that distinguishes it as a brand.

Another challenge to retail comes in the form of e-commerce. For the time being, Din remains confident that it does not pose a major threat to traditional fashion retail. The Internet remains limited. It is not only slow but it is unenticing. Browsing on the Net is a frustrating and solitary activity. Its most successful application has been by retailers such as supermarkets who sell essential commodities, whose customers are saved the time and inconvenience of visiting a store; book and CD sales are also booming, since they can be easily selected by title or category. In fashion retail, however, Internet shopping has largely remained an adjunct to mail order. For Din, only once it has parted ways with the PC and found its way into the centres of our homes – into our living rooms and on to our TV sets – will the killer e-tail format arise. Then it will become

a focus for social interaction and leisure activity. It will also be far more conducive to finely targeted marketing. Din gives the example that in a few years time it might be possible to find out exactly who is interested in a particular range of goods through the programmes they tune into or request. A family watching programmes on camping will receive information on tents and outdoor equipment, for example.

What is certain is that retail has become a business environment where even the established giants, such as Marks &Spencer, cannot remain complacent. The goal posts are not only continually moving but are being reinvented. A retailer cannot expect to be only a retailer. The onset of participatory retailing means that, as well as selling goods, stores are having to set themselves up to provide all sorts of services. DIY stores, for instance, are now offering car hire so that customers can easily organise taking home that enormous new sideboard that won't fit in their Ford Fiesta. To be sure of payback for investment, shopping centres, department stores and individual shops are having to compete for the disposable incomes in their customers' pockets – keeping them within their shopping environment as long as possible. There are 40 restaurants, bars and fast-food outlets contained in the Bluewater Shopping Centre alone. Selfridges in London has created eateries in line with the luxury branded goods it sells. Even designer shops such as Nicole Farhi are bringing more people in with restaurants within their stores. If architects are to compete in this specialist area which requires an up-to-date knowledge of marketing, they are going to have to learn to participate and, ultimately, to facilitate. ⚙

New Retail is published by Conran Octopus (London), 2000.

chitecture

An interview with Sally Mackereth

For young architects, fashion has a powerful allure. It offers a glamour and visibility on the street that is second to none. Sally Mackereth of Wells Mackereth Architects – a rising practice based in London – is prepared to be candid in her enthausiasm. She told Helen Castle of *Architectural Design* just how fascinated she is by the industry. Having designed three Jigsaw Menswear shops in the north of England, the office has recently completed a highly innovative fit-out for the Italian company CP Company & Stone Island in Beak Street, Soho.

Above
Sally Mackereth of Wells Mackereth.

Right and opposite
Wells Mackereth, Jigsaw Menswear shop in Leeds, completed late 1997.

'Disposable, ephemeral and fickle' are the words most often applied to fashion, emphasising not only the speed at which it moves but also the industry's notoriously short attention span. Though Mackereth has no illusions about the business's transience, her references to the fashion industry are peppered with richer, more baroque imagery. To her, the relationship between fashion houses and architects shares all the complexities, and no doubt intrigues, of the relationship between the great patrons of the Renaissance and the creative talents they employed. She opens our conversation with an analogy between today's most powerful brands and the Catholic Church – both dominant and all pervasive, their influence extending across global cultures and borders. The enormous budgets the brands channel into refitting shops, the most conspicuous display of their wealth and power, has historical precedents in the huge expenditure of royal families, political figures and religious institutions. She talks of the rivalry between LMVH and Gucci in terms that would do justice to the 16th-century Borgias. She likens Rem Koolhaas' recent commission by Prada to that of the Medicis' relationship with Michelangelo and their quintessential marriage of style and power.

Mackereth, however, regards the dynamic behind fashion itself as the key to understanding the success of many celebrity architects, such as Koolhaas and Herzog and de Meuron. Fashion works on a personality basis: each fashion house is identified with its own named designer whether it be Donatella Versace, Stella McCartney or Tom Ford. These designers set the tone of the lifestyle message to build the particular brand. The brand's values are carefully generated, fiercely controlled and guarded by the fashion houses themselves. The association of a specific architect at a given time with a designer gives unqualified added value to a brand. For instance, Calvin Klein was adamant that he wanted to commission John Pawson, the architect who would share his design approach and philosophy. The spare minimalist look of the stores that Pawson created for Klein became as integral to the fashion house's identity as the clothes themselves.

As with royalty, the public and private personas of these celebrity fashion designers often become merged. The interiors of their own houses, often designed by the architects of their stores, are widely published in magazines and broadsheet supplements, further propagating the brand lifestyle message. In the last few years, fashion companies have caught on to the popular demand for designer products by extending their ranges to branded homeware. It has now become possible to take a little bit of Donna Karan home with you in the form of a vase or bedlinen. Essential to this marketing exercise seems to be the coveting of objects and products that are attached to the palpable image of a particular individual – their looks, their values, their

world. Mackereth likens this trend to the vogue for scaled-down versions of Louis XIV's Versailles gardens of 18th-century Europe – Louis symbolising decadance, frivolity and opulent style rather like Galliano for Dior today.

Contemporary fashion cannot be contained only in the garments we wear. Where you shop and what you surround yourself with have also become a means of expressing certain values and attitudes. In our overpopulated, increasingly urbancentric world, brands express tribal allegiances. Fashion is now more than ever about a level of indulgence, which expresses status, kudos and 'belonging'. It enables people to mark themselves out from the anonymity of the city and align themselves with a particular group. Clothes and brand accessories can thus become a way of outwardly displaying that you are in the 'know'. For fashion houses, retail space has become an essential medium for the promotion of these defining brand values. Unlike the clothes themselves, it is not limited to the extremities of the human body. Mackereth maintains that a spatial skin offers the potential for a far more engulfing and engrossing physical and visual experience than that of mere clothing. As the trend for shopping online increases, so the power of three-dimensional space in the form of a retail outlet created as a sensory experience for the shopper increases in importance for the powerhouse brands. For retail design, the architect is able to shape and form the space using contrasting materials, light and drama to create a journey of theatre and illusion.

While fashion is by its very nature contradictory and transient, architecture is about permanence and longevity.

Mackereth believes it is better for architects tackling retail design to embrace and enjoy the fact that they are dealing with what is essentially disposable space. In her opinion, they need to instill the same sense of event and thrill of occasion in their architecture as there is in a 20-minute catwalk show.

Mackereth's regard for the sensuous is reflected in her approach to her own work. Wells Mackereth is arguably more catholic than other Modernist practices. It uses unlikely materials in unconventional ways. For the recently completed bar and restaurant, Smiths, it has employed the soft luxury of cashmere on sliding doors to contrast with the rough brickwork of existing warehouse walls. PVC strip curtaining introduces a further textile and texture. Super-scale leather banquette seating in the champagne bar gives Cadillac luxury to an otherwise raw, basic space. In its design of the CP Company and Stone Island store in Soho, Wells Mackereth worked with German product designers Zeichenweg to create a laddish, techie ambience in keeping with the urban outfitter's range of products – casual sportswear made in high-tech materials. The practice made sure that the clientele, who take delight in buying a jacket with earphones embedded in its hood or a coat that turns into a tent, would be able to experience the same versatile wonder in the retail space. The most conspicuous of these features are the fibreglass rods or light sabres, designed by Zeichenweg, which create a grid for the clothes rails. Plugged into sockets on the floor, they can be reassembled flexibly in various configurations to alter the shop display. The sockets are controlled by a panel, or 'navigator'. This is playfully high tech, with large Flash Gordonesque buttons and wires. Similarly a double-height magnetic wall allows shelves to click immaculately into position as required. Though Wells Mackereth cannot take full credit for the use of the light-rod system (it was also used for CP Company's shop in Milan), its adaptation into the architecture is artful. The openness of the shop, with the stairs positioned at the front pulling customers downstairs, does not allow the gadgetry to dominate or clutter the space.

Certainly the CP Company and Stone Island's shop demonstrates just how fruitful an understanding of the client and their products can be. Mackereth is unstinting in her belief that good client/architect relations are at the core of successful architecture. For her, the role of the architect and the client has remained much the same throughout history. It is a matter of finding a working dialogue and establishing a creative dynamic. Though a professional relationship, it is also inherently personal like that of a doctor and patient, with the patron often referring to the architect in possessive terms. Like the Medici family and Michelangelo, perhaps Miuccia Prada is talking about Koolhaas as 'my' architect. Δ

FASHION ART
IN NEW YORK

From the street in New York's SoHo, all you can see inside the Yves Saint Laurent Rive Gauche Homme boutique is a gigantic, shiny, red rhinoceros ready to charge customers entering the store – if it is a store. Lettering on the window says it is, as does that on the old-fashioned awning. But you have to climb a short flight of open, steel, industrial stairs before you really see any clothing. The glass front door leads into a gallery for temporary art shows, now completely filled with Xavier Verbehiel's big beast.

The exquisitely arranged garments are around the corner in a dematerialised space where scrims veil walls lined with classical cast-iron columns and teasing screen-hanging racks.

Only a few years ago, the streets of this 19th-century industrial district were lined with real art galleries. Today, most of them have moved a mile or so north to a more barren area in West Chelsea, where warehouses and garages still coexist with the growing art scene – dozens upon dozens of galleries and residential lofts apartments for art collectors, dealers and fashion people. Gluckman, now practising as Gluckman Mayner Architects, has recently done stores for Helmut Lang in SoHo, Gianni Versace in Miami Beach and YSL Homme in New York and Paris.

While other New York architects – Deborah Berke, Frank Lupo and Daniel Rowen, David Piskuscus (of 1100 Architect), Michael Gabellini, Rogers Marvel, Tsao & McKown – were developing their own versions of Minimalism in the mid-1990s, Calvin Klein hired John Pawson to design his flagship store on Madison Avenue. At one stroke, the shop established an emerging trend on the city's swankiest shopping street and made the most celebrated retail outlet of the 1980s 12 blocks north (which happened to belong to Klein's main competitor) seem slightly old-fashioned. Of course, the French Renaissance Revival mansion that Ralph Lauren had turned into a $14 million, 28,000-square-foot fantasy (with designer Naomi Leff) was supposed to be old-fashioned. It offers shoppers a chance to enter the Gilded Age, wandering from parlours where accessories are strewn across sofas into bedrooms where sweaters are stacked

A global fashion capital, New York takes its place alongside London, Paris, Milan and Tokyo. Since the Second World War, however, the metropolis has also been the centre of the international art market. Jayne Merkel, editor of New York's *Oculus* magazine, reveals how in Manhattan fashion has followed contemporary art. It has shadowed the relocation of galleries within the city, emulated its architecture and design and even started incorporating exhibits and installations within its own shop floors.

with bare concrete floors, concrete walls, concrete ceilings, exposed ducts and industrial light fixtures.

It all began at the end of West 22nd Street where New York architect Richard Gluckman, who designed the YSL SoHo store, transformed a 40,000-square-foot warehouse into the DIA Foundation's non-profitmaking exhibition space in 1987, creating a taste for the Minimalist aesthetic he had developed over the years when working with collectors and artists such as Dan Flavin and Donald Judd. The architect went on to design galleries all over New York and museums around the world, and these in turn influenced younger architects who were also designing galleries, photography studios, retail stores and in closet-like niches, while they suit themselves out in the trappings of lineage. But once Pawson's study in abstraction (complete with Donald Judd furniture) opened, nostalgia suddenly seemed less stylish. The Calvin Klein store, which was perfectly attuned to the plain, structured, monochromatic goods for sale, seemed more classically up-to-date. Its 34-foot-tall windows are set between two-storey Ionic pilasters on the base of a 1927 bank. Inside, Pawson painted everything white, covered the floors with stone from his native Yorkshire, smoothed out all surfaces and built crisp, rectangular niches (with tubular, stainless steel, right-angled racks for clothes) in the three-storey shop to emphasise the 20-foot-high ceilings and large blocks of unobstructed open space.

Opposite
Christian de Portzamparc's Louis Vuitton Möet Hennessy (LVMH) Tower. A symbol of fashion's globalisation, it is also a testament to the quality of French luxury goods.

Now stores up and down Madison Avenue are stripped to the bone – Peter Marino's Emporio Armani, Roberto Baciocchi and David Foley's Prada, Timothy Greer's Krizia, Antonio Citterio's Cerruti, to name only a few. White, black, stainless steel, glass, mirrors and marble are ubiquitous. And so are LED screens flashing TV-like images, as though they were somehow unusual. In part, the trend is sparked by fashion itself – plain pants, plain jackets, T-shirts, all-black wardrobes. But it has also been affected by store design, gallery design and the fact that Minimalism has been the strongest direction in New York architecture in recent years, garnering the majority of awards in professional competitions, even though the public remains obsessed with historic preservation and most Americans choose neotraditional design for their own homes. The preference for the past is so strong that the art and design worlds have come to define themselves in opposition to it, as have those who want to appear avant-garde. And, not surprisingly, their numbers are growing now that new technology is changing the way we live and making a lot of people fabulously and instantly rich.

New York, however, has never been a very technologically oriented town. In the late 19th and early 20th centuries, when heavy industry made the United States a force to be reckoned with, New York's main product was clothing. The city's economy is based on trade, finance and publishing (now media). After the Second World War, however, New York also became the centre of the international art world, and the garment industry evolved into a design centre. When mass-produced retailing edged out couture, Seventh Avenue became as influential as Paris, though most sewing shops moved first to the American South and later to Asia. The part of west midtown Manhattan that used to be called 'the garment district' is now officially known as 'the fashion centre', and that is not just a euphemism. The real economic power in the garment industry now comes from design and marketing. At a panel discussion on real estate pressures in the garment district last spring, the CEO of Nicole Miller, Bud Konheim, said:

> People talk about the garment centre as if it were one thing. There are two or three different kinds of businesses. I have very little to do with the guy making 12,000 things for Wal-Mart. I need to be near the Italian mills, which have offices here, and be accessible to the buyers. New York has become a centre of design innovation … we have to be in an art centre to be creative. You cannot do this in a field in Iowa. You don't get the buzz. Businesses based on design need to be here; those based on price don't.

His attitude provides another reason why retailers moved to SoHo and why stores drew inspiration from the architecture of art. Richard Gluckman isn't the only gallery architect working on boutiques today. Deborah Berke, who is designing new studios and galleries for the Yale Art School, designed Club Monaco on lower Fifth Avenue and the prototype for CK jeans. 1100 Architect created spaces for Metro Pictures and J Crew. Rogers Marvel designed the Studio Museum in Harlem and a series of shops for Kate Spade.

Daniel Rowen who, with his former partner Frank Lupo, designed a number of galleries and a widely published all-white Minimalist apartment for an art dealer, was engaged by Michael Kors to design his first retail store. But from the beginning, Rowen knew he wanted to take a different tack from Gluckman's. Before he put pencil to paper, he set off for London and Paris with his wife and Michael Kors' creative director to look at historic shops, check out the competition and spend some time in hotels and restaurants that Kors himself frequents. 'It was a way of developing a collective visual reference,' he said. Charmed by Charvé, impressed by Michael Gabellini's Jil Sander Paris and convinced that he wanted his prototype to reflect Kors' particular sensibility, he decided to make the new store on the corner of

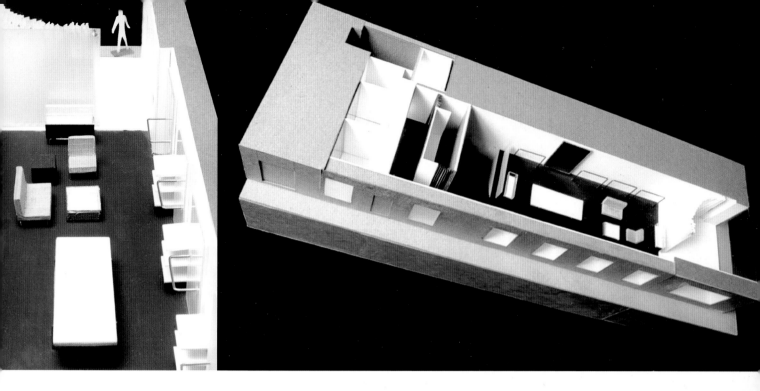

Above
Daniel Rowen, model of
new Michael Kors shop
on the corner of Madison
Avenue at 76th Street.

Madison Avenue at 76th Street a kind of salon but not an art gallery.

A series of small boxes set into the 76th Street facade showcases individual items. Even the storefront will not reveal the interior or the collection. A single mannequin, surrounded by a circular curtain made of silk, wool, or wire mesh (the materials will rotate), can be seen from the glass facade in a kind of foyer. Inside, on dark wood floors (to ground the space) Florence Knoll furniture rather than fixtures, reflecting Kors' abstraction of form and reduction of materials, creates the sense of a luxurious salon. The most lounge-like spaces are in the basement, where salespeople bring customers for fittings or special showings. As in many boutiques today, the sales desk is hidden. Financial transactions and wrapping will take place in the back of the house. The sensuous quality the architect seeks distinguishes the all-white apartment he designed with Lupo and is evident in his offices for a Zen publishing house, also in New York. Both interiors almost float.

Sensuality of one kind or another is showing up in what may be the next wave of retail design. It is certainly what makes Michael Gabellini's work stand out. The veined golden marble sales desk in his Searle store at 605 Madison glows from within. At the new Nicole Farhi on East 60th Street, there are organic-looking carved wood racks instead of the tubular stainless-steel ones standard in the neighbourhood; the main floor hovers over an underground restaurant.

Another kind of energy is at work in Janson Goldstein's DKNY sports shop at Madison Avenue and 60th Street. Although it has Minimalist detailing (a polished concrete floor, white walls, cubic forms and exposed ducts), there is a spirit of too-muchness, which is not particularly typical of the architects' work. (Their new store

for the florist Bloom has the quiet, residential feel of Rowen's design for Michael Kors, and an almost Japanese serenity.) At DKNY, there are natural wood boxes, glowing Plexiglass boxes illuminated with coloured fluorescent tubes like those Dan Flavin used, intensely coloured niches and LED screens flashing everywhere. This cacophony is consistent with the Day-Glo merchandise and the views of the colourful street scene, which is visible on two floors. Since the centre of the corner store is opened with a wide-angled staircase, vertical movement is visible too, creating an atmosphere almost antithetical to that across the street at John Pawson's Calvin Klein, where plain staircases are tucked into corners behind walls, street views are obscured, whiteness prevails, materials are limited and details are extremely refined.

Somewhere between these two extremes is the Cerrutti shop at 789 Madison (near 67th Street) by Antonio Citterio and Partners. Here too, the palette and detailing are severely restrained (big sheets of glass on the facade, more plain stainless-steel racks), but there is a stark contrast between the very dark brown wood floors and the crisp white walls, a contrast echoed in the black-and-white photographs from old movies on the walls. This shop, though small, also extends over three levels, but the staircase is in the rear, perpendicular to the side walls. It, too, is quietly detailed—with thin strips of stainless steel inlaid in the wood. Like many New York stores, Cerruti occupies a single 25 x 100 foot floor lot on the pervasive New York grid, which was divided into segments suitable for terraced houses in 1811. For retail purposes, however, the ubiquitous shape provides only limited street frontage and natural illumination.

Architect David Ling had the same kind of space to work with at Philosophy on West Broadway in SoHo. He extended it vertically, too, with a staircase at the back of the store. But here, the entire two-storey facade is glazed (with panels subdivided by stainless-steel strips) and nearby buildings are low, so the interior is

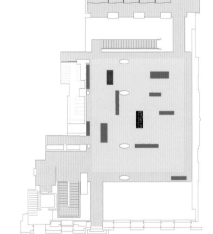

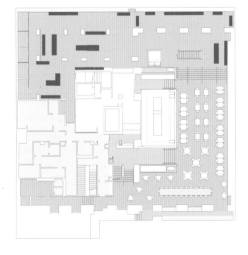

Above
Gabellini Associates, Nicole
Farhi. The main floor area
hovers over an underground
restaurant.

Right
Plan of Nicole Farhi, New York.

filled with natural light which flows through glass floors, glass partitions, a glass case around the stairs and a glass balcony railing – all edged in stainless steel. The constantly changing light creates a certain sensuality, as does an organically curved black wood reception desk and a matching conical element that extends through the second floor to penetrate the ceiling on the first. Despite the big glass facade, only one or two garments are visible from the street, on headless mannequins in the window. Racks of clothing are tucked into rectangular niches along the side walls or displayed on glass shelves out of view. Retailers these days put window-shoppers on a strict diet. There are no feasts
for the eyes. Even browsers can only snack.

For the gluttonous, there is Christian de Portzamparc's Louis Vuitton Moët Hennessy (LVMH) Tower – 25 floors of luxury goods wrapped in folds of faceted glass. Sadly, only the first floor of the elegant slender tower, which pierces the skyline fetchingly on East 57th Street, is open to the general public, and that space – a store for Christian Dior – is less subtle than the building as a whole. The glittering tower itself with its multitoned skin (ultraclear, low-iron glass, heat-strengthened vision glass, sandblasted glass with a line pattern, green glass, clear and silkscreened in tiny dots) snubs its nose at Euclidean geometry, cutting back to meet New York zoning setback requirements cleverly. It curves round, folds over and slopes down to create a scintillating profile on a 60 x 100 foot site between the equally narrow, rectangular, 17-storey Chanel Tower and a bulky 15-storey office building with a classical colonnade on top, in the shadow of Edward Larrabee Barnes' huge, angular IBM Building across the street. But instead of ending in a peak, LVMH tops out with a three-storey glass box housing a 'Magic Room' for parties and photo shoots, hovering in the nest of Manhattan towers. The most beautiful and innovative skyscraper built in New York since Mies van der Rohe's Seagram Building, de Portzamparc's glittering tower is a symbol of globalisation, an apt testament to the quality of French luxury goods and a savvy answer to the American preference for bigness.

The Christian Dior store, designed by Peter Marino of New York, is more indigenous. It is Minimalism with a make-up job. A series of glossy, glassy rooms *en suite* enfolds along the axis of the deep, narrow interior, which occupies only the eastern half of the site. But the glass

shelves here, unlike the plain ones in most other shops, are edged with bronzed, gilded or silvery ridges, and glass display tables have thin, angled, metal legs. Although casework is tucked into niches, as it is in more restrained stores, the lighting is more stagey. Mirrors encourage vanity, too, especially on the staircase which has grey and silver carpeting with a leopard-skin pattern, and silvery metallic railings shaped like branches of a gnarled tree. As in other emporia, the decor suits the wares inside. This is not the Dior of my mother's youth. Denim halter-tops with shiny CD buckles and motorcycle jackets with frilly skirts would probably make poor classic Christian turn over in his grave, but they do suggest a playfulness that is showing up in several other areas.

It appeared a few years ago in a delightful town house conversion for Moschino on Madison at 64th Street by set designer Piero Capobianco of Los Angeles and Adam D Tihany of New York. Taking cues from Milanese Modernism, Surrealism (especially Miró and Magritte) and pop culture, they turned the store into a funhouse with sparingly used bright colours, spiralling curves and witty murals. The 'Toy-lette' off the children's department is wallpapered with Lego. If somehow you failed to notice Moschino's slightly weird sense of humour, the decor proclaims it.

Less giddily, but with a similar sensitivity to the clothing designer's gentle wit, Toshiko Mori and Gwenael Nicolas created a tiny shop in SoHo for Issey Miyake. Translucent film turns the large windows on two walls into aqueous now-you-see-it-now-you-don't peepholes.

A few steps down Wooster Street, a three-year-old store by the team of young architects at SHOP (Sharples Holden Pasquarelli) of New York for the Italian owners of Costume National is wet-looking in a very different way. Here, the look is slick as streets shining after the rain. And it's perfectly suited to the sleek black jackets and trousers hanging along the side walls on tubes. Everything is black and white, or rather, shiny black (floors, ceilings, walls with a very high shine) and translucent, glowing, bright white (Plexiglass boxes lit from within, hanging from the ceiling, on the back wall, standing on the floor and set in the window as bases). Cantilevered acrylic shelving lit with fibre optics projects some garments into the dematerialised space, and spotlights emphasise the materiality of the clothing sparsely hanging from the tubular racks. Absolute symmetry reinforces the rigour.

A few blocks east of SoHo, in a growing area of small new designer-owned boutiques called Nolita (north of Little Italy), on Elizabeth Street, SHOP recently completed an assertively asymmetric and softly finished little jewellery store. The boxes reappear, but here, at Me & Ro, they are varied in size and set within walls, one of which is deep red. The boxes become display

Right
SHOP's store for Italian
designers National Costume
in Wooster Street. The look
is wet and slick – streets
shining after the rain.

cases for the intricate handmade objects. A lily pond made of cast-in-place concrete supports the large storefront glass and draws people into the store in a manner consistent with the designers' sensibility.

The direction that these young, increasingly prominent architects are taking may suggest the near future of retail design. For the first Museum of Sex (MOSEX) in the United States, to be built on Lower Fifth Avenue next year, they designed an occupiable skin composed of undulating layers of translucent, coextruded, polycarbonate, acid-etched Starphyre glass, Teflon-coated fibreglass panels and flat-lock zinc panels. A composite steel frame made of I-sections and interwoven, custom-rolled steel tubes will support the 36,000-square-foot, six-storey building. SHOP's winning scheme for a competition sponsored by the Museum of Modern Art and PS1 for the courtyard of that non-profitmaking art centre in Queens last summer was a continuous surface that bent and folded to become an urban beach with a cabana, beach chair, umbrella, boogie board and surf. It rose to offer shade, descended to provide inclined seating, turned on its side to create changing areas behind a translucent veil. Water ran along it, shimmering, forming pools, and turning into mist.

The partners at LOT/EK, Ada Tolla and Giuseppe Lignano also rising stars in New York who were finalists in that competition, recently completed an art gallery in Chelsea that further suggests a breaking of the Minimalist mould. Drawing on that raw tradition, the architects, who always introduce found objects (like old

truck beds and TV screens), inserted a 10-foot-high continuous band of wallboard into a former parking garage on West 20th Street to create the Sara Meltzer Gallery. The white band, which reveals the construction system of light metal studs and gypsum board, is cantilevered from the perimeter walls so that it floats in the space without touching the floors or ceilings, which remain visible above and below. At certain points, it detaches to define spaces for a reception desk and storage. Cuts along the skin generate windows, casings for fluorescent lights and little bookcases projecting from the outer wall. Additional lighting fixtures, pipes and ductwork on the ceiling are, of course, exposed, but after the entry over the old metal grate of an automobile ramp, everything seems edgier here.

A hint of a new day in West Chelsea appeared last autumn when the first boutique opened. Granted, it was Comme des Garçons, which had moved into SoHo before most galleries and was fleeing the area, as they were, to avoid the shopping-mall atmosphere. The dramatic new store is located in a former automobile shop with the sign, 'Heavenly Body Shop' still on the old brick wall. The entrance, through an existing arch, leads into an organic-looking steel tunnel, past a pivoting door and explodes into a strikingly white space. The inside is almost completely plain except for a large curved, freestanding wall and the sparely displayed clothing, designed, like the shop itself, by Rei Kawakubo who worked on this space with the Japanese architect Takao Kawasaki and New York's Studio Morsa. Without Future Systems' entry sequence through metallic entrails, the ethereal interior might seem Minimalist. As it is, the glowing whiteness seems a world away from the DIA Foundation down the block, where the trend and the trendy district all began.

SoHo is still flourishing. It still has galleries on the southern edge and on upper floors, but it's predominantly residential now with shops and restaurants on the ground floors of old renovated industrial and commercial buildings. And the newest, most outrageous one symbolises the change. Shoppers who come upon The Apartment, on back-alley Crosby Street just below Prince Street, can see in through a big picture window or peer voyeuristically through the front door's reverse fish-eye lens peak hole, but once they step over the glowing cast-glass doormat (with the name of the store instead of 'Welcome' embedded in it), they may come upon occupants quarrelling or snuggling on the couch, a dream kitchen

(designed by Marc Sadler for Boffi) complete with a cook ready to make them a snack, and everything else they'd expect to find in a hip duplex SoHo loft. The couple who 'live' there are a pair of actors who drop by from time to time to do a performance piece. The cook is a chef from Le Gamin, a café nearby; she serves crepes, sandwiches and salads that visitors can eat at the glass-topped dining-room table a few feet away. In the living area, above a Marcel Breuer sofa, old movies are playing on a state-of-the-art Audiophile Home Theatre System, with a plasma screen TV by Sony Style hanging from the ceiling. The usable lavatory with Philippe Starck fixtures has a turquoise poured-epoxy floor, like the ones the architects (Belmont Freeman of New York) install in the laboratories they design.

Down a stark steel-plate staircase with cast-glass treads, a bedroom with exposed brick walls and concrete floors has clothing and works of art hanging from old water pipes, new exposed galvanised steel ductwork, a desk with used books, designer stationery trays, even a retro (Macintosh Classic) computer ready for use. And everything is for sale. Even the pebble-lined bathroom floor, Ann Semonin spa-line bath, and

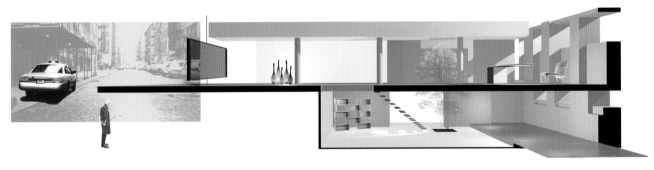

Jayne Merkel is the editor of *Oculus*, the magazine of the AIA New York Chapter. She is also on the editorial board of *Architectural Design*. She has recently completed monographs on the New York Office of Richard Dattner & Partners, and Pasanella + Klein Stolzman + Berg. She directed a graduate programme in Architeture and Design Criticism at Parsons School of Design, and has taught art history at several other colleges. She has writtten for *Art in America*, *Artforum*, *Architecutre*, *Progressive Architecture* and numerous other publications. She was also the architecture critic for many years on the *Cincinnati Enquirer*.

freestanding Starck shower, which customers can try out if they dare. The floor is kept wet to suggest that someone did. The merchandise in the shop, which was designed by Monty Freeman and Lynn Herlihy of Belmont Freeman Architects, will change every month – or be rearranged as if The Apartment belonged to a mad perpetual decorator. Actually, it 'belongs' to mad shoppers. You can drop into The Apartment any time (www.theapt.com).The owners – the husband and wife team of Wharton Business School graduate Gina Alvarez and independent film-maker Stefan Boublil – travel the world shopping for merchandise not available elsewhere in the United States. But they have taken care to ensure that The Apartment doesn't look too precious. It's a little messy, with the lived-in look of a real loft that could belong to the trendy young heirs of the Madison Avenue mansion where Ralph Lauren created a very different kind of fantasy not so very long ago. But it seems like another century (which, of course, it is). Δ

Yves Saint Laurent
Rive Gauche Homme
New York

Gluckman Mayner Architects

Richard Gluckman started designing exhibition spaces in the historic cast-iron district of New York's SoHo during the 1970s, long before he or it was famous. After the New York Earth Room for Walter de Maria's earth work and a permanent gallery for the same artist's *Broken Kilometer*, in the 1980s he went on to design galleries, for the dealers Mary Boone and Larry Gagosian, which changed the way in which art was shown in New York. Instead of upstairs loft spaces with bare brick or white-painted walls and rows of thin classical cast-iron columns, like most galleries in SoHo at the time, these were garage-like ground-floor sheds with skylights and doors resembling those of aeroplane hangars.

By the mid-1990s, SoHo had become so popular that retail chains started moving in, forcing many galleries out. Designers with an avant-garde following still wanted to be there, but not in traditional stores. Enter Gluckman. At the Helmut Lang boutique at 80 Greene Street, two racks of garments are displayed like art in the window. Once inside, the customer encounters several large sculptures and a site-specific light sculpture by the artist Jenny Holzer. Other artists – Donald Judd, Richard Serra, James Turrell – are there in spirit through their influence on the architect. In the back, beyond a room-dividing, translucent glass wall, is the main retail area with four black box cabinets, containing the designer's collections, facing away from the door and a long, low table for sales and wrapping along one side. Across

the street, Gluckman's even more minimal new shop for Helmut Lang Parfum sells only four fragrances in a deep, light-filled box with a central display island and another pulsating Jenny Holzer sculpture.

In the next block, at 88 Wooster Street, Gluckman's Yves Saint Laurent Rive Gauche Homme has an art gallery in the front for temporary shows. And since the shop is half a level above the street, no clothes are visible there. As in the Helmut Lang boutique, the collection is displayed in the rear, along a single row of cantilevered T-shaped racks and on two 30-foot-long glass counters. Sheer white scrims divide the display space, veil the side walls and cast-iron columns, and diffuse the natural and artificial light. Clothing hangs perpendicular to the side walls between scrims and is arranged on stainless steel drawers with green glass tops along the sides. The sparsity, strict rectangularity and lighting together create a very, very quiet space.

In YSL in Paris, on the Place Saint-Sulpice, Gluckman used a scrim as a backdrop for hanging garments in one wing of a V-shaped space, where it is flanked by aluminium cabinets; a curtained area at the end accommodates special showings and displays. In the other half of the V, along the Rue Bonaparte, that plan is inverted. Racks run along the perimeter, and the centre is filled with a monolithic aluminium display bar. A curved hall, lined on one side by backlit, aluminium-framed, translucent fibreglass cladding, connects the ends of the wings and provides an entrance to the lounge and fitting rooms at the crook of the V. Here, however, in the tradition of French luxe and history, the whole store is more delicate and refined than its American counterparts. ⌂
Jayne Merkel

Gabellini Associates

Jil Sander
Office and
Showroom
Hamburg

Architects who first become known for retail design usually have trouble breaking out of the mode. New York-based Michael Gabellini is the exception. Though he gained recognition for Jil Sander stores soon after he opened his office in 1991, he went on to design installations for the Guggenheim Museum and the Cooper-Hewitt National Museum of Design in New York. His work was featured in the first Design Triennial at the Cooper-Hewitt earlier this year, along with that of Richard Gluckman, Steven Holl, Tod Williams and Billie Tsien, Greg Lynn and other leading designers. Gabellini first met Sander in 1982 when he designed the Linda Dresner store in New York, the only place where her clothes were available at the time. Sander asked him to do the boutique she opened in Paris on the Avenue Montaigne in 1992. Then she purchased a war-damaged 19th-century villa in a park on the banks of Hamburg's Alster Lake and asked him to convert it to an 18,000-square-foot office and showroom. The architect reconfigured the historic rooms upstairs, restored plaster reliefs and woodwork, and waxed the plaster to emphasise its texture. He also designed starkly modern new lighting, furniture and fixtures to go inside and installed a new Spanish Arria floor to tie the restored spaces together with modernised ones on the lower level. They are connected by a grand flight of existing stairs leading up from the foyer and brand-new, light, angular ones going down to meeting and dining rooms with an outdoor terrace.

The Jil Sander and Ultimo Showrooms in San Francisco are also located in a landmark building where Gabellini Associates created a cool, disciplined, monochromatic space for the Jil Sander collection and a rich, sensuous,

colourful one for Ultimo; the two spaces are interlocked around elliptical columns. Whereas Jil Sander's showroom is light-filled and double-height, visually fading away at the edges, the Ultimo store is housed in a red chinoiserie box with a vaulted ceiling, silicone bronze walls, a backlit marble backdrop, silk scrolls, mirrors and hand-carved furniture by George Nakashima.

Gabellini also used Nakashima's furniture and organic-looking carved hang bars in a store he recently completed for Nicole Farhi in New York. The main shopping floor, paved with sanded slate and attached only at sides, hovers over a restaurant and a housewares department on a subterranean level. The entrance over a wooden footbridge emphasises the floating quality.

The architect's new 60,000-70,000-square-foot store for the 25th anniversary of Giorgio Armani in Milan, however, is earthbound and tied into the city. This miniature galleria with a public passageway running through it, a café and a whole market full of shops purveying 'the Armani lifestyle' has a cruciform plan.

The firm have also executed a showroom for Jil Sander in Milan. Its latest venture for Sanders, however, is a 10,000-square-foot shop in the dramatic two-storey, skylit banking hall of the Royal Bank of Scotland in London, where fashion week shows have been held in recent years. The building, which the bank purchased in 1933 and vacated two years ago, was orginally built as a residence for the Earl of Damley in 1721, expanded by John Vardy Jr in 1785, and purchased by the Bank of England in 1875 when the hall was added. Here, at the corner of Burlington Gardens and Saville Row, Gabellini is emphasising the building's unique historic decoration and achieving the serenity customers have come to expect through effective lighting and by maximising on the spaciousness of the interior. ◌ *Jayne Merkel*

Issey Miyake

Pleats Please
New York

Toshiko Mori Architect

If the tantalising little shop on a busy commercial corner in New York's SoHo looks both serenely simple and surprisingly complex, it is because the architect has not only been designing special little stores for almost 20 years, but also because she has been doing research on materials, experimenting with their effects and studying immateriality in architecture. Toshiko Mori designed a much-celebrated shop for Comme des Garçons at Henri Bendel in 1982, Comme des Garçons Shirt, on West Broadway in SoHo a few years later, and a showroom and earlier store for Issey Miyake on Madison Avenue with structural fibreglass as thin as one-eighth of an inch all while teaching, first at the Cooper-Union where she was trained, later at Yale and now as a tenured professor at Harvard.

On Pleats Please she collaborated with Gwenael Nicolas, a graphic and product designer who works for Miyake in Tokyo and Paris. Instead of trying to lure in the streams of tourists who now trudge past this busy commercial corner, they decided to tease them into entering. First, they removed the tiny, obstructed windows in the simple 1852 brick tenement, preserving the cast-iron supports between them but removing some brick to create larger openings. Then they inserted a new glass box just inside the thick masonry walls, an approach that appealed to preservation officials for the landmarked district. They coated the window glass with a colourless adhesive polymer film (Lumisty Film) that veils the interior from some perspectives and offers glimpses into it from others, just like water in an aquarium. The continuous floor-to-ceiling glass liner (which is recessed to create appropriate shadow lines at the pale blue window casings) blurs the edges of the 600-square-foot shop, turning the entire interior into a slightly surreal chamber which is rendered even more mysterious by a shiny, headless, bright green mannequin in the window. The glass provides translucence and reflectivity as it passes over openings and over the opaque, painted wall (a very light green); the veil of film disembodies the space further, severing connections between inside and outside.

Time stands still in the interior, where the beautiful-but-strange pleated garments tantalise further, and a shiny bright green box-within-a-box contains the sales desk, which, due to the little stainless steel legs on which it perches, does not make the shop seem cramped. Glass casework on the white limestone floor intrudes only minimally. It is difficult to gauge the size of the space as a dropped ceiling in the centre and the filmy windows blur reference points. Ambiguity, of course, is the name of the game and attracts customers whether or not they know what to expect inside. The shop at 128 Wooster and Spring streets opened in 1998 and still invites onlookers who tend to retrace their steps as they pass, trying to fix a clear view.

Like the architects of other extraordinary stores in New York, Mori has designed spaces for art as well as fashion. In 1994 she designed the Louise Nevelson wing of the Farnsworth Museum in the late artist's home town in Maine, and a renovation of an old mill for an art foundation in Georgia is currently in design. Last winter, her experimental woven shelters for victims of earthquakes, famines and wars were exhibited at the prestigious nonprofit Artists Space in SoHo, and her installation for the Museum of Modern Art's recent exhibition of Japanese textiles, 'Structure and Surface', is currently touring. ⌂ *Jayne Merkel*

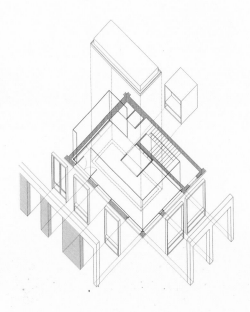

Rei Kawakubo of Comme des Garçons

In May 2000, Rei Kawakubo received the Excellence in Design Award from the Design School at Harvard University. This acknowledged her unique contribution to fashion since founding Comme des Garçons in Tokyo in 1972, as well as her excursions into other areas such as furniture, interior and theatre design. The award was made with particular reference to the vision that she has shown in guiding the architectural design of the Comme des Garçons stores. Here, in a short extract from his presentation speech, Jorge Silvetti, Chair of the Department of Architecture at Harvard, pays tribute to her.

There is an immense amount already written about Rei Kawakubo's work, which tries to 'interpret' and give it meaning. This has, in general, only been contradicted or changed by her own further moves. She unequivocally rejects any fixed interpretation of her work. On the rare occasions that she has spoken:

She has denied that her work is art.

She has disassociated her work from any particular 'message' that people may see in it.

She has discouraged any association between 'politics' and her work.

She has insisted that there is no hidden agenda in her design work.

And, so, for instance, she has repeated that it is futile to try to find a message, a political or artistic agenda. This is expressed in the strange, unconventional name she chose for her company, Comme des Garçons or 'like the boys' – she just liked the way the French sounded.

What she wants to know is whether you like what she does or not, and of course, she would prefer that you do.

What she wants to do, emphatically, is never repeat what she has done before. To quote her: 'I want to design clothes that have never yet existed. I do not wish to design anything similar to my past works, either. I must be a rebellious person.'

With this in mind, let's go back to our criteria for the award. Rather than being based on a set of pre-established rules, they've evolved in an ad hoc manner which has allowed us to adjust and calibrate our moves. Established in 1997, the Graduate School of Design's Award is still young. It has only had three recipients – Philippe Starck, Robert Wilson and Rei Kawakubo. Only now is it beginning to display a composite, unique profile vis-à-vis other design awards.

It is not about one design piece. It is not about a 'lifetime achievement'. It is not about discovering emerging talent. It is about proven genius with a substantial productive career still ahead.

It rewards creativity and success (two issues necessarily intertwined in the fields of design).

And finally, it is about true, real, breakthrough innovation in any, some, many, or all aspects of a design field, in ways that transform the field itself.

While this general profile has clearly emerged, its application to the specific field of fashion has proved more difficult. When rating creativity for example, how do you define and evaluate it in a field that is propelled by forces that require designers to come back every season with new designs? All of them. Is it then just a matter of degree? Specifically, take 'breakthrough innovation': how do you measure it in a field that works on articles that are as old as man, with work being repeated over and over again on the same items? Or, how do you establish what constitutes design work that effects a transformation of the field itself?

The inherent difficulty in tackling the set of criteria in fashion became easier and easier as our discussions progressed. As we attempted to clarify each issue at hand, Rei Kawakubo's name kept cropping up. Indeed, she exemplified everything we thought the award in fashion should be.

And again, eschewing any direct interpretation of her work as I promised, I will continue to be 'objective' and report on its effects. First let's enumerate her 'objective achievements':

She 'invented' black as a colour. She challenged our perception of the beautiful. She has subverted received ideas of how women should look and liberated them from the duty of looking 'beautiful' every day. She revolutionised and changed for ever the dominance of the traditional 'fashion' show and its ritual standards, right at its very centre, in Paris.

She has given old materials radical new dimensions. She has pioneered and introduced new techniques and materials in her work. She did not name her design lines with her own name. True to herself, in a field defined by the 'signature' of the designer, she has been constantly inventive.

Because of all this, she has never left the fashion press indifferent. She has been called many things, notably: formidable, shy, notorious perfectionist, control freak, revolutionary, fashion anarchist and God's gift to fashion.

In a field that epitomises the designer as ego, and where competition is fierce, the reaction of Kawakubo's peers to her work is telling: either silence, which is in itself a form of recognition, or explicit recognition, which comes in two forms, direct or indirect testimonials. Of the first John Galliano: 'I'm in awe of her discipline, I like the way she's always pushing and exploring.' Azzedine Alaia: 'In 1993, Rei brought novelty and change to fashion at a moment when it was most needed. I am moved by her work. After 12 years of showing in Paris her work remains in the vanguard, and each new collection becomes in its turn a source of inspiration for the future.' In short, the young Alexander McQueen, Jil Sander, Donna Karan cite her as the world's most gifted designer.

Perhaps the most important testimonial to her achievements is the indirect recognition that she has received through other designers' work.

Her influence has been absolutely ubiquitous throughout the fashion industry. Every one of her moves has penetrated the field over time. To be more specific, one of her most radical innovations – the deconstruction of garments – now finds expression in the work of Martin Margiela, Helmut Lang, Ann Daemeulemeester. Her reinterpretations of techniques or uses of materials, such as synthetics, have invariably had an even broader impact, going beyond the field of fashion design.

Indeed, after each season's presentation, Rei's designs have shifted over the years from being initially shocking to intellectually enlightening about our culture. Enriching sources of aesthetic inspiration for other designers, they have brought about substantial technical, procedural and advertising modifications of the industry.

Finally – as if we needed more proof of her genius – when we decided to exhibit her work here, and we offered our services, as architects, to design the exhibition, she decided to design it herself. We obliged. The evidence is outside these doors.[1] It is as if she decided to apply everything she does to clothing to architecture. We have been given back, as it were, our building, transformed into a new experience. The exhibition has reconfigured the gallery space, and for those of us who have spent more than a decade in it, it has been rendered into an experience that we never imagined possible.

For all of this, I would like to offer you, on behalf of the Harvard Graduate School of Design, the year 2000 Third Excellence in Design Award. Δ

Notes
1. Silvetti was referring to the exhibition of Kawakubo's work, 'Comme des Garçons: Structure + Expression', on display at Harvard Design School Gund Hall Gallery, 4–31 May 2000.

jas group architects in collaboration
with Woolf Architects, 1998

ADOLFO DOMINGUEZ

Adolfo Dominguez
Manchester

Right
The front of the Adolfo
Dominguez on John Dalton
Street, Manchester. Three
shop windows are grouped
around the door.

Above
The rear of the store, which
backs on to a small square,
with a central shop window
and logos to either side.

Juan Salgado's design for a Spanish fashion designer's store in Manchester has an indisputably European feel. It was his use of the store's particular local context and site, however, that helped him to communicate this continental brand effectively to Mancunians.

The main aim of this project was to give the Spanish fashion designer Adolfo Dominguez a presence in Manchester. The third outlet in Britain, it is the first shop outside London. Though Juan Salgado, a young architect from the same town in Galicia as Dominguez, had been involved in the Regent Street store, the Manchester one was his first major retail design. Adolfo Dominguez is a small brand here although it is well known in Spain and Salgado seized the opportunity to give the logo optimum impact by transforming it into an architectural symbol. The shop is in many ways a testament to the architect's ingenuity. Salgado made the existing retail space, located on the ground floor of a seemingly uninspiring 1970s office block, work not only for him, but also for its site, squeezed between a square at the rear and the entrance on John Dalton Street. As a foreigner, he took the opportunity to look at the city with fresh eyes, choosing to optimise Manchester's warm blue light and long hours of winter darkness in his design.

Previously a computer-software shop with retail space on John Dalton Street and offices at the back, the Adolfo Dominguez shop was designed so that it penetrated the whole shell. This had obvious benefits for the interior space, but also for the exterior. A continuous facade was wrapped around the corner of the building. Three shopfronts were placed near the entrance and a central shopfront on the rear elevation. This gave the volume as a whole far greater transparency – an important quality in such a grey,

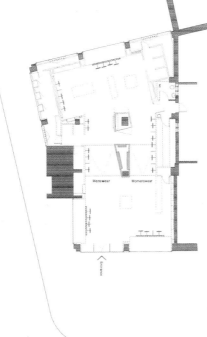

Above
Rear and side of store.

Right
Floor plan of store.

Far right
On the side can be seen
the chequerboard of cubes,
which mirrors the niches
that are a standard fitting
in Adolfo Dominguez stores.

Opposite top
View of interior from back
of store showing the two
new elements that Salgado
created out of the structural
columns.

Opposite bottom
Plan of central unit or element.

Menswear   Womenswear

Entrance

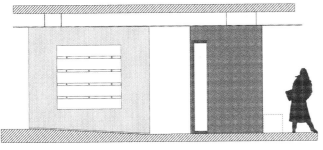

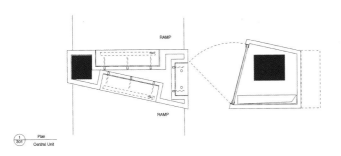

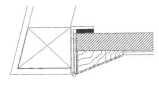

monolithic structure. It was, however, the frequent use by office workers and shoppers of the urban square at the back of the shop as a pedestrian thoroughfare that allowed Salgado to redistribute the shop's point of focus, generally reserved for the front elevation, to the side and the rear. At the back, a glazed block protrudes out flush with the facade. It is divided into three equal sections, with a central shop window, and the left and right sections have black backing and light boxes built into the wall, illuminating Adolfo Dominguez's logos. These emphasise the monolithic stone cladding and bring the shop to life after daylight hours. This is particularly effective in the winter months, when people cross the square on their way to work in the dark and return home after dark.

The side wall elevation also creates an important focal point, as an axis between the front and the rear of the store. Designed as a chequerboard of cubes for displaying accessories, it mirrors the niches that are a standard shopfitting behind the counter in Dominguez's other shops. This not only sets up a relationship with the vocabulary of existing shops, but also makes a connection with the display of products in the interior.

Inside, two existing structural elements necessitate a lengthways division of space; a division that is underlined by the separation of the shop floor into menswear and womenswear areas. By wrapping the elements around the structural columns, Salgado effectively integrates them into the architecture of the new store. The first element is used to open up the view of the store and stretches the length of the ramp, which Salgado introduced to replace some steps in the old shop. The other element is used as a display unit for accessories. These two volumes thus become an efficient architectural solution for easing the split between the two floor areas and for creating showcases.

Opened in November 1998, the Manchester Adolfo Dominguez store was produced in a four-month design and construction period. This left the architect very little time in which to manoeuvre, since he had a 12-week construction contract. Salgado wryly observes that the slowness of architecture and its construction runs contrary to the contemporary condition of the fashion world. What is apparent, however, is that in spite of the race for completion Salgado was cannily able to establish a foreign brand image through a number of small architectural interventions, which also drew heavily on their local context. ⬭

This article is based on an interview with Juan Salgado.

ca.com.mx

Stores for Aca Mexico City

Jonathan Bell describes Mark Guard Architects' design for a chain of clothing shops in Mexico City – an exciting departure for a small, London-based practice with no previous experience of fashion retail.

Retail design is rarely sympathetic to an architectural approach. In a world where the customer is king, large-scale retailers could be forgiven for their dependence on off-the-shelf solutions, insipid design and a general cautiousness. But occasionally, the status quo is overturned, and a client is found who is willing to encourage and embrace a radical solution. John Pawson's work for Jigsaw and Calvin Klein, Nigel Coates' designs for Katherine Hamnett and Jigsaw, and the bespoke retail environments created by firms like Din Associates have all eschewed the traditional shop form in favour of ascetic, simple lines or a bold approach that is not afraid to challenge the conventional view of the shop. For the most part, however, retail detail is formulaic, relying on standard components with the occasional detour into Disneyesque showmanship to draw in the crowds.

London-based practice Mark Guard Architects specialises primarily in private residential work, and has very little previous retail experience. The practice was therefore surprised to be approached by the American owner of a chain of clothing shops in Mexico City. The client, who had seen their work featured in a coffee-table monograph that focused on the refined thread of reduced Modernism for which the practice was known, had come to London in search of a similar aesthetic for the comprehensive rebranding of his existing corporate image. From the outset the client, whose Aca Joe stores have an extensive presence throughout Mexico City, was open to new ideas.

Architect and client underwent an exhaustive analysis of clothing stores, travelling from Fifth Avenue to Bond Street, as well as to Mexico City and the recently opened Bluewater Centre in Kent. In many ways, the megasprawl of Bluewater provided a mirror of the Mexican model, despite the former's semirural setting. Mexico City is one of the largest urban centres in the world. Its very newness means that instead of being a series of interconnected villages or towns, it is based on radial growth from the centre. Despite a built-up area of 1,500 square kilometres, the metropolitan area of Mexico City is some 4,500 square kilometres (compared with Greater London's 1,578, with Inner London only 321). Some 17 per cent of Mexico's total population of 100 million live within this endless horizon of suburbia.

Left
Aca store in Durango
department store, Mexico City

Mexico City's shopping zones are predominantly based on the American mall model, rather than the traditional high street. Security problems are prevalent – there is a high incidence of violent crime – and malls are perfect for middle-class shoppers, being climate-controlled, security-patrolled environments that can be reached by car. As well as the mall outlets, in locations such as Santa Fe, Polanco and Durango, several of the Aca Joe shops are in department stores. Chief amongst these is the large Palacio de Hiero chain, which can be found throughout Mexico City, as well as the curiously named Liverpool chain. These large stores tend to anchor the covered malls, providing points of entrance at each end of the covered streets of smaller shops.

Mark Guard Architects decided to reduce the components of the standard Aca Joe shop to a few simple elements – a clean aesthetic that would be strong enough to take the various alternative approaches required. The previous stores featured heavy wooden shelving and high stacks of clothing. The new design eschewed this 'woody Western' look. Instead, they were

composed from a series of integral components – a long, wenge wood table for serving, displaying, purchasing and wrapping goods; a poured concrete floor that flowed, unbroken, throughout each unit; independently lit wall shelving; recessed wall hanging; several freestanding metal shelving units; and one large photographic image. Plaster walls and ceiling are painted white and the rear wall of each store is clad in backlit etched glass. The wood table, raw concrete floor and metal boxes all provide a tough, almost utilitarian aesthetic to contrast with the clothing on display. The poured concrete floor is inlaid with a stainless-steel grid, providing the geometry to frame each of these quite disparate elements, unifying them and allowing each store to become a composition – an alternative arrangement of identical elements. As Mark Guard points out, there is also a sound commercial reason for allowing such flexibility: the components can be rearranged within each different-sized unit in order to provide a consistency of appearance, yet also maximise the amount of available space for selling.

The rebranding of Aca Joe to Aca also included the integration of Internet sales into the stores, a move that corresponded with the launch of a website to sell clothing online. Each store provides space for one or

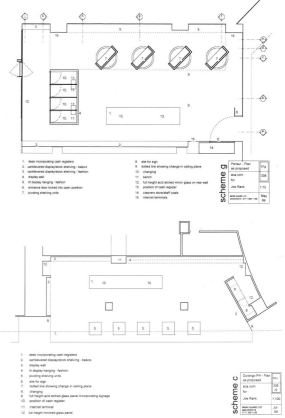

two Internet terminals, allowing customers to view, select and purchase items once they have seen them in the flesh. The clothes can then be dispatched either to their home from the central warehouse (if they are out of stock, for example) or as gifts to friends.

Initially, freestanding rotating metal shelving units were designed as an integral part of the space. Each rotating unit could be used to alter the appearance of the shop from a 'clean' aesthetic to a 'busy' one, perhaps occasioned by a special promotion or a seasonal sale. Likewise, the long wenge wood table can either be kept clear of stock or used as an additional display space as and when required. While this 'transformable' element drew on Guard's experience of creating solutions for domestic living spaces, these 2-metre-high rotating metal units were considered too bulky for the smaller outlets in the department store and so 1.2 metre metal cubes were designed as replacements, used for knitwear display.

The design manages to maintain an overall identity for each store, despite the varied sizes, shapes and locations of the units. While the basic 'kit of parts' provided elements – long table, concrete floor, display units, photographic image and shelving – that could be manipulated to fit the various units, the 'floor grid' also facilitated the unification of each space. In department store concessions, this change in floor finish was crucial, providing a visual and tactile cue to customers that they were entering a separate, and quite different, kind of store. In addition, the backlit glass wall acts as a beacon, catching the customer's attention from across the crowded shop floor.

Both architect and client have acknowledged the need to understand consumer psychology, occasionally at the expense of sacrificing some of the more elaborate design gestures (such as the rotating units). The design is not prescriptive – the stores can be clean or cluttered as commercial demands dictate. However, the overall emphasis on a clean aesthetic is both highly designed and modest – the customer should only notice the clothes. The result is a chain of stores that is far removed from the standard identikit shops, shoehorned into unsuitable spaces, that often characterise malls and department stores. The meeting of architecture and commerce need not be a compromise.

The reconstruction of the shops was undertaken in collaboration with the Mexican architect Luis de Regil. ∆

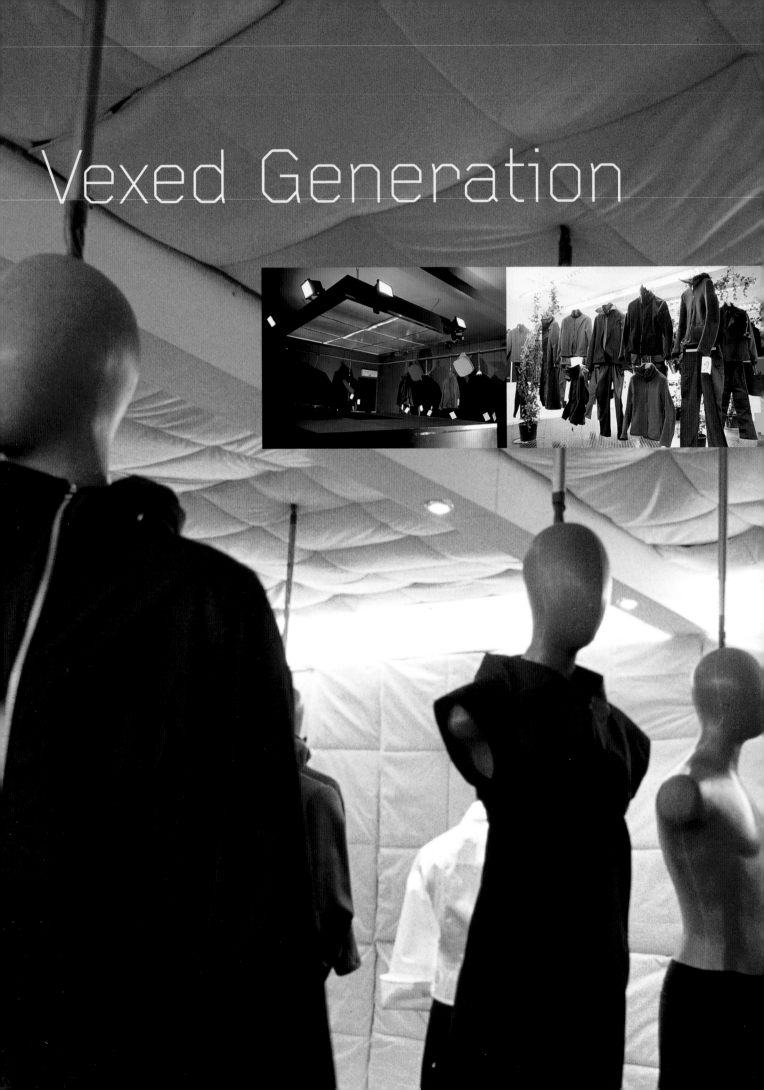

Vexed Generation

It is not the architectural world alone that is taking the lead in innovative retail spaces. Vexed Generation is a small London fashion house that invents exciting and creative themed environments to accompany its edgy, urban designs. The creation of its own ephemeral retail sets is a means of bypassing the catwalk and taking its work directly to the public.

Opposite page, inset
Left
'The Green Shop' in 1996/7,
Vexed Generation's second
store located on the first floor
of 3 Berwick Street in
London's SoHo with 'breathing'
walls.

Right
'The Grow Room' 1998/99, the
third Vexed Generation
installation was located in the
same retail space as 'the
Green Shop'.

Opposite page, main
'A Stitch in Time' (detail)

Above left
For 'A Stitch in Time'
1999/2000, same space as 'the
Grow Room'. Visitors
encouraged to draw on the
walls.

Above right
The first Vexed Generation
installation opened in 12
Newburgh Street, SoHo, in
1995. Taking London's street
environment as its inspiration,
its front window was whited
out and its interior was placed
under constant surveillance
rather than being staffed.

This article is based on an
interview with Adam Thorpe.
Vexed Generation will open a
new location early in 2001.

Adam Thorpe and Joe Hunter of Vexed Generation have been designing and retailing unique clothing products since their inaugural collection in 1995, which included the much-copied one-strap bag.

A small, independent operation, Vexed chose not to show its clothing via the conventional catwalk show, but rather to invest its ideas in a more permanent retail installation, combining creativity with commerce, and allowing both press and public to experience the collections and concepts first-hand rather than through the filter of media and buyers' opinion. Vexed collaborates with designers, artists and musicians to create the spaces in which to display and retail its collections.

The first Vexed retail installation, opened in 1995, sought to create an environment reflecting the collection's design brief: London's street environment in 1994/1995 – surveillance versus society, rights and responsibilities, air quality, civil rights. Since the front window was whited out, passers-by could only view the interior via a small monochrome TV screen. The interior space was under constant surveillance. The curved, backlit walls displayed statistical information relating to the social and ecological urban environment. The floor was of white gravel. This provided easy maintenance and

alerted those who entered to a 'change in space' from the street outside. The clothing was displayed in a glass case in which holes were cut to allow visitors to touch and view the garments but not remove them. A key aspect of the installation was the absence of 'staff'; only if you ventured downstairs would you find the Vexed crew within the public access gallery beside the record decks and 'alternative TV service' made up of combined video works from the public.

Shop 2, 1996/7, was The Green Shop. Located on the first floor of 3 Berwick Street – down an alleyway, along a dark corridor and up a spiral staircase – it continued the environmental theme. Clothing was displayed on inflatable bags that, linked to an air compressor, inflated and deflated on a timer, giving the impression of 'breathing clothing and walls'. The open-access gallery and decks were located in the changing area and counter respectively.

Shop 3, The Grow Room, saw the garments arranged in rows in the centre of the space. Fast-growing plants such as ivy, clematis and passiflora grew up through the clothing, sprouting from armholes and neck openings, an optimistic reference to the strength and adaptability of nature. The walls were lined with blackboards inviting people to enter their personal details, an experiment in public/private access to information. The floor covering was comprised of £750 worth of one-penny pieces, an example of safety in numbers: you can leave hundreds of pounds on the floor in small coins and not worry that they will be removed. People may also contribute new pennies, thus producing a 'wishing floor'.

In Shop 4, A Stitch In Time, incorporating 'The Label Database', the downstairs corridor moved towards you as you entered. It was in fact a water ramp, whose trickle of water was reflected around black glass walls. Brush-matting flooring on the staircase and display area dried your feet as you approached the changing/gallery area, where your footprints were taken on a Plasticine floor. Moving walls increased the display areas and could create separate spaces for changing. Clothing was displayed on mannequins, some standing, some suspended over a black glass floor which reflected the padding on the ceiling and walls on which people could record their presence in thread. They could also print a name label and sew it on to the wall, creating a textile database of customers and collaborators. ⬩

Egg

Hidden away in a series of mews houses in Kinnerton Street in Knightsbridge is Egg. A highly idiosyncratic clothing shop for men and women, it is sought out by an international clientele who come to enjoy its unique artistic and domestic ambience. Asha Sarabhai explains how she and her partner Maureen Doherty developed the idea.

Egg emerged from a shared and essentially common sense philosophy, which allowed space to capture the sense of wonder in a statement like 'Think the colours of the peacock emerge from a white egg.' With no disrespect to 'experts', it was felt more important to have a congenial, welcoming space where people could exchange – be it thoughts, frocks or pots.

The existing spaces in Kinnerton Street, stripped back, voiced their own inclinations. Number 36's cool dairy blue tiles and cobbles stayed as did the exposed 'sheet' pipes (to the distress of certain austere architects). Working with a friend, interior designer Frankie Cole, the principle was to keep the spaces as organic as possible to maximise flexible use. The natural light of the space was a great asset too. It felt appropriate to evoke the intimacy of a home and the sense of an open market place where dropping in for a chat, tea or a Moscow Mule and a look around was a pleasure. A place of exchange and circulation.

The clothes and objects themselves are primarily concerned with ways of making and doing rather than with names and branding. They are not about experts dictating what's in fashion, more about presenting an alternative, based on years of experience and a particular point of view. It is an attitude akin to contemporary tradition, which risks assuming that there are others who might share an affinity with it. It's more about quiet resonances than grand statements. Or to put it another way – at the risk of sounding absurdly neo-existentialist – the register is more 'I be, I be' than 'I am, I am'.

Interest and fun remain vital. You never know what to expect at Egg from one week to the next – an art installation of cabbages and kings, a window display of a hundred milk bottles or a student from the Royal College of Music playing the cello. The idiosyncrasies of a group of people at work and play are what make Egg a moving kaleidoscope. ᴁ

Yes, We Wear Buildings

The relationship between fashion and architecture doesn't stop at fashion retail. There is a long tradition in Western culture that has likened architecture to clothing. Karen Franck examines this metaphor, and even dares to suggest – contrary to the edicts of the modern movement – that architecture may be fundamentally linked to fashion.

Wrapped, smooth, fluid, transparent, layered, material, border, sleeve, exposed, texture, fold, facing, pattern, decorative, fabric, ornament, veiled, fluted, fastened, patch, stiff, cosmetic, worn, reveal, covered, hung, formal, symmetry, cut, foot, fussy, elegant, measure, size, image, model, sketch, design, style, seam, coat...

The metaphor of architecture as clothing dates back to Vitruvius and possibly earlier.[1] In more recent history, architects in the modern movement turned to clothing again and again both for a positive and a negative analogy. The goal of modern architecture could be likened to a change in clothing: to shed the overly fussy, decorated dress of the 19th century and to don a plain coat of pure white.[2] Even though clothing as an explicit metaphor is not as popular as it once was, the continuing overlap of terms suggests a deep commonality between building and clothing – in experience, ideas and design. The words used to describe clothing are themselves a source of architectural design ideas ('fold', for example), as are actual ways of dressing (such as Itsuko Hasegawa's inspiration for the Asajigahara Rest Area, Nara Silkroad Expo, Nara City, 1998)[3] Both buildings and garments are made by hand and machine to enclose and yet display the human body in all its physical, cultural and psychological dimensions. Each is an extension of that body. Each touches and is touched, seen and felt.

Okay, clothing but who wears it?
With their curves and fluidity, their layering and transparency and their variety and richness of materials, some buildings today may remind us of clothing. This is building-as-clothing that is seen or worn only by someone else. For in all the modernist talk of architecture as clothing it was always an 'other' who wore it. It is not recorded that any of the architects who designed clothing in the modern movement ever designed it for themselves (or for any other men). Less literally speaking, the body that occupied the clothes, even the much admired English suit (an early model for modern architecture) was always the over-there or object body, never the here or subject body.[4] The architect was outside – outside the space, outside the garment – gazing at it, never occupying it himself.[5] Thinking of architecture as clothing can reintroduce embodiment and lived, sensory experience into architectural discourse and education, but only if the designers/writers/readers 'wear' the buildings themselves, feeling, as well as seeing them. This would be a significant and much-needed change from the modernist tradition, still in force, which makes the architect a detached observer and which privileges vision to the exclusion of other senses.[6]

Clothes that we wear on our bodies, that we feel and move in, that we care for and become attached to, bring us to the possible intimacy of architecture, to where it 'touches' us in so many different ways. It is no longer out there in front and at some distance, a sight/site only for the eyes and the intellect. It is instead all around us, whether we are indoors or out, giving us feelings and sensations, encouraging us to move in certain ways and not in others. Being within the space says something, as clothes do, about who we are and who we wish to be. And we may develop strong feelings of attachment, associating a building with experiences we had there so that, like a favourite dress or jacket, it becomes part of a personal history. While the connections between building, identity, and memory are particularly strong for houses, this is also true of public buildings.[7]

When architecture becomes clothing of the here body, the one I am as I write this and the one you are as you read, sensory experience becomes alive and immediate. How will it feel to open the door or the window? And what of the floor? What sounds will I make as I walk? What sounds will others make – children in a library, people with walkers in a nursing home? What will it feel like to touch the handrail, to grasp it and slide one's hand along it? What size and shape, material and finish will give it those sensations? What are the many sensations of sound and scent and touch and movement that are desired for occupants in this particular building?

Many of the answers are found in materials, which can be selected for their sensory qualities.[8] In clothing design, material is not secondary to form but an integral part of it. The drape that is sought is made differently by velvet and silk, so is the sound and the temperature generated by each. Heating, cooling, ventilating move from being only technical questions to experiential ones as well. The cover image of Lisa Heschong's classic book *Thermal Delight in Architecture* is not a building but a straw hat.[9] Thinking of buildings as clothing we wear brings the living, feeling, remembering body into the building. It also links use, construction and care to aesthetics. The lesson Peter Blake suggests for new architecture students is also in a hat, the *ngob* from Thailand, 'that absolutely flawless example of the interplay of form, function, light, texture, structure and economy of means … so modestly presented, so totally devoid of critical or academic double talk'.[10]

Many straw hats recently made in Europe and the US can be folded and packed, without breaking or loosing their shape. And think of the detailed directions written on clothing labels today: 'turn garment inside out, machine wash cold, tumble dry low, warm iron if needed' or 'dry clean only'. If architecture

Above
Frank Gehry, Guggenheim Museum, Bilbao (1997).

Right
Itsuko Hasegawa, Asajigahara Rest Area, Nara Silkroad Expo, Nara City (1998).
'… the Muslim kurta, the Iranian Chador and the Indian sari. The image I had in mind … was of a group of people in such a dress; but I also wanted to suggest nomadic tents, pao … and the mountain ranges along the Silk Road.'

is clothing we wear, issues of care and durability over time and use come to the fore, becoming design concerns with consequences long after the building is photographed and publicised, after it is well worn. For, unlike a lot of clothing today, the building is not easily discarded when it shows signs of wear, has been outgrown or is out of fashion.

No, not fashion. Never? Oh come on.
The relationship of architecture to fashion is more problematic and more contradictory than the architecture as clothing metaphor. Associated as it was with the feminine, the frivolous, the irrational, the misleading and the sensory, 'fashion' captured all the values modernism sought to reject. And yet Frank Lloyd Wright, Otto Wagner, Henry van de Velde, Peter Behrens and Josef Hoffmann all designed dresses for wives and clients, and the worlds of art, architecture and fashion were closely intertwined in avant garde circles in Europe. As Mark Wigley demonstrates in *White Walls, Designer Dresses*, contemporary texts on modern architecture as well as subsequent histories carefully omitted these aspects, presumably to avoid any taint of fashion.[11]

In cultural studies, fashion is generally denigrated while food, lifestyle and popular music all arguably as transitory and frivolous are not.[12] Elizabeth Wilson also points out that the denigration of fashion for its consumerism sees only its oppressiveness.[13] Yet fashion, like architecture, is a key physical manifestation of culture. Both translate a dream into material form and offer that dream to people to clothe and represent their identity. By wearing the clothes fashion has produced, by occupying the buildings architecture has made, we inhabit the dream. In wearing the clothes, or approximations of them that are affordable, may we not experience pleasure, beauty, power and self-confidence? Is it not possible that 'wearing' the building, even as a one-time visitor, can stimulate similar feelings?

The rejection of fashion by the modern movement was also fuelled by a rejection of its rapid change and its emphasis on appearance. This is curious considering that what was being advocated was exactly such a rapid change in architecture and its appearance. Indeed, one could reverse the equation and see the parallelism: both modern architecture and fashion sought the appropriate look for their time. Is not that what architects do today as well, whether they are designing retail establishments, schools, museums or churches?

The linkages and cross-fertilisations that do occur, unavoidably, between architecture and fashion are invaluable

to each; pretending otherwise or decrying this as a weakness on the part of architecture is an old and censorious position. Why not fully acknowledge the conditions that do exist and examine the present or potential relationships, exploring both the benefits and the drawbacks that ensue, as this issue of △ begins to do? The 'commercialisation' and overt fashionableness of architecture, as found in the design of restaurants, stores and hotels, not only represents a significant portion of contemporary architectural practice but also brings its potential enjoyment to a much wider public than the architecture of private homes or even public institutions. Perhaps it is precisely that enjoyment, the possibility and pursuit of pleasure with all its sensual qualities, and the perceived threat to architecture as serious, that is the true fear. △+

Karen A Franck is a professor at the School of Architecture and the Department of Humanities and Social Science, New Jersey Institute of Technology. Her most recent book is *Architecture Inside Out* (Wiley-Academy, 2000), co-authored with R Bianca Lepori.

Opposite
Itsuko Hasegawa, Shonandai
Cultural Centre, Fujisawa City
(1989).

Far left
Steven Holl, Kiasma, Museum of
Contemporary Art, Helsinki (1998).

Left
Steven Holl, door to Kiasma,
Museum of Contemporary Art,
Helsinki.

Below
Nils Ole-Lund, 'Architecture
of Fashion', from *Nils-Ole Lund:
Collage Architecture*, Ernst and
Sohn (Berlin), 1990.

Notes
1. Mary Mcleod, 'Undressing Architecture: Fashion, Gender and Modernity' in
Architecture: In Fashion, Deborah Fausch et al (eds), Princeton Architectural Press
(New York), 1994.
2. This point and the following historical references to modern architecture and
fashion are taken from Mark Wigley's work, *White Walls, Designer Dresses: The
Fashioning of Modern Architecture*, MIT Press (Cambridge, Mass), 1995 and from
Mary Mcleod, op cit.
3. Hasegawa Architects, *Itsuko Hasegawa*, Academy Editions (London), 1993, p 57.
4. For differences between these two kinds of bodies see Don Ihde, 'Virtual Bodies',
Body and Flesh: *A Philosophical Reader*, Donn Welton (ed), Blackwell Publishers
(Oxford), 1998 and Karen A Franck, 'It and I: Bodies as Objects, Bodies as Subjects',
Architectural Design, no 136, 1998.
5. For further discussion of this condition and its alternatives see Karen A Franck
and R Bianca Lepori, *Architecture Inside Out*, Wiley-Academy (London), 2000.
6. See Juhani Pallaasma, *The Eyes of the Skin: Architecture and the Senses*,
Academy Editions (London), 1996.
7. See Clare Cooper Marcus, *House as a Mirror of Self*, Conari Press (Berkeley),
1995.
8. See the chapter 'The Animism of Architecture' for exploration of the qualities of
materials and 'From the Body' for a discussion of posture and movement in Karen A
Franck and R Bianca Lepori, op. cit.
9. Lisa Heschong, *Thermal Delight in Architecture*, MIT Press (Cambridge, Mass)
1979.
10. Peter Blake, *No Place Like Utopia*, WW Norton (New York), 1993, pp 330-331.
11. Mark Wigley, *White Walls, Designer Dresses: The Fashioning of Modern
Architecture*, MIT Press (Cambridge, Mass), 1995.
12. Elizabeth Wilson, 'All the Rage', in Jane Gaines and Charlotte Herzog (eds),
Fabrications: Costume and the Female Body, Routledge (New York), 1990, p 28.
13. Op cit, p 53.

A Critical Contribution

Charles Jencks and △

Since 1977, Charles Jencks has been △'s most regular contributor. As well as consistently producing influential articles, he has guest-edited individual issues and been instrumental in the staging of △-related events. In an interview with Helen Castle he describes how, over a period spanning three decades, △ has been a critical catalyst in important architectural debates. During the 1970s and 1980s, both △ and Jencks were inextricably linked with Post-Modernism, but they also turned their attention to classicism and deconstruction. By the mid-1990s, Jencks was once again fuelling discussion with a special issue on science, and △ was shifting its focus to cyberspace.

CJ: I came to Britain in 1965, partly motivated by the fact that there was a strong architectural movement going on here. It was led by two magazines: *Architectural Review* and, particularly, *Architectural Design*. △ was a forum for architects such as the Smithsons, Team Ten and their friends, and for architectural thought – Ken Frampton, importantly – and a series of architects who were later collected in a book called *British Architecture*.[1] In one sense, it was the mouthpiece of the modern movement in the 1960s, and an important reason why I came to Britain.

By the late 1960s, △ had started, as British architecture had, to become extremely confused and to go into anti-architecture. The confusion between hippies, the May events, antiformalism, and being against design (which paralleled the art world) meant that △ lost its previous direction. But it found a new one as a polemical young magazine. That was the period when it was associated with the Architectural Association, where I taught, and particularly with Alvin Boyarsky and the summer school through Robert Middleton. That period was very dynamic and international. Although it was not oriented to the modern movement per se, it was critical of it in many respects – you could say it was at the heart of what I called Late Modernism.

In any case, that went on for a few more years under Monica Pidgeon, until 1974 or so. Then there was a transitional period where, both in its production and in its layout, it lost its readership and its dynamism. It was printed on cheap paper.

Then it was picked up by Andreas Papadakis around 1976. For two years, Martin Spring, Haig Beck and others were interim editors and part-owners.

The Post-Modern Period 1975–87
HC: Didn't you write for △ before then?

CJ: I wrote little articles, but only snippets. It was much more oriented than I was towards High Tech, and throwaway architecture. The first issue I put together was done informally. First of all, in 1975, Andreas Papadakis asked me to write a book, which later turned into *The Language of Post-Modern Architecture*. It came out in 1977. While I was working on that, we produced an issue that I organised, partly because I knew Arata Isozaki. It was the January 1977 issue. That created the first new look of △ – the Post-Modern △. My article was called 'Isozaki and Radical Eclecticism', and I showed that he followed many different approaches, not just the Modernist approach. He himself said that he made mannered versions of different architects – Renaissance, Baroque and modern – but they were always creative; they were not pastiches. You could see that Isozaki was an important leader of the Post-Modern movement, as indeed was Hollein and Americans such as Venturi and Moore.

If I may talk about my own contribution for a

moment, what happened was that in 1977, *D* became closely associated with the Post-Modern movement; in fact, it became a world mouthpiece for Post-Modernism. In May 1977, we produced an issue around my book with other authors from America, particularly Bob Stern, Paul Goldberger – the critic from the *New York Times* – Charles Moore and others. I would say that from 1977 to 1985, *D* was focused mostly on the Post-Modern. Parts of my books on Post-Modernism were reprinted in it. First, in 1980, was an issue of *D* called *Post-Modern Classicism*; then there was a follow-up to that, *Free-Style Classicism*, in 1982. Those two issues showed that Post-Modernism had focused on a free-style version of the deep language of architecture rather than a revivalist classicism. These issues started a movement within Post-Modernism, although it was a large umbrella, like Modernism, that included other approaches. It became a large movement in philosophy and art, as it had been in literature. It became a cultural formation in that period. By 1983, I had produced a third issue in the series, *Abstract Representation*, which was the latest transformation of free-style classicism. Hans Hollein was on the cover – and you could see a lot of Michael Graves' influence in that, as well as Eisenman, Robertson, Japanese architects, people like the Venturis and Stanley Tigerman. Then we did issues for *D*'s sister magazine, *Art and Design*, on the Post-Modern Object and Post-Modern Art. As the Post-Modern movement became successful, after its high-point in 1984 (with the opening of Jim Stirling's new Staatsgalerie in Stuttgart), we also published critical issues coming out of debates that we had organised. For instance *Post-Modernism on Trial*, which I organised in 1990, discussed the dilemma 'Between Kitsch and Culture'.

HC: So, after Disney, you were reacting against a backlash against Post-Modernism?

CJ: Yes. I was critical of the way that, in their work for Disney, Michael Graves and Robert Stern were appropriating kitsch. Basically, the Disneyfication of Post-Modernism brought out its worst aspects. Yet there were architects, such as Hans Hollein, who were making their peace with commercialism in an inventive and contextual way, such as Hollein's Haas House in Vienna, which we published. And there was the interesting urbanism of Robert Krier and Aldo Rossi. So there was the continuity of Post-Modernism into the 1990s. We did a whole *D* issue on London called *Post-Modern Triumphs in London* in 1991, with an exhibition in a derelict modern tower in London – a Post-Modern rehab. In that issue, you could see 80 or 100 Post-Modern buildings. What had started off as a trickle in

1977 had become a flood, and a lot of it – more than 60 per cent – was pretty awful. But that was not as bad an average as Modernism had produced in the 1960s: about 90 per cent of that commercial version was just dreadful. A point I have continuously made is that most everyday building is rip-off architecture, produced at too high a speed for too little money. These forces have eroded every movement in architecture since 1800. They have all been destroyed from within. So what else is new? Of course, Post-Modernism was one of these and, having predicted it, I then criticised the debacle.

Another issue we produced in 1987 was *Post-Modernism and Discontinuity*. You can see on the cover a funny mixture of characters. The painting by Karl Loubin shows Andreas Papadakis, the publisher, talking to Jim Stirling and Jim Stirling, talking to Leon Krier; James Gowan, Terry Farrell, Fenella Dixon and me, all set within Jeremy Dixon's new opera house. That gives you an idea of the way Andreas saw Post-Modernism. You can see that with the Dixon and Jones building it is becoming close to a revival of the classicism that Leon was promoting. We also published in this issue the Clore Gallery of Jim Stirling, and Terry Farrell's urban work. Farrell, of course, became the most famous London practitioner of Post-Modernism.

Deconstruction and History
HC: You punctuated that with other things, such as deconstruction, and then you moved on.

CJ: Yes. Three issues on deconstruction were adapted from my book *Architecture Today* and expanded. With book publication – and I don't just mean mine – Andreas' point was to make every shot count twice. Partly, this was because *D* was published on a shoestring, and it was the only way to survive.

HC: But it was also telling, because it means that everyone wanted to see what was going to come out, and they were prepared to buy a magazine about the book because there was that much excitement. You can't just do that on nothing, can you?

CJ: No, you have to have a movement and a polemic to do it with, and that's why *D* was always so good. Since the 1960s, at least at its best it has always been polemical – fast moving and quick reacting. For instance, at short notice, I got Bruce Goff to come over

This title of △D featured a specially commissioned painting by Kan Loubin. In the foreground are depicted some of Post-Modernism's best known protagonists, while in the background is a view of Dixon and Jones proposed design for the new opera house. *Post-Modernism and Discontinuity, Architectural Design,* vol 57, no 1/2, 1987.

to Britain to give a talk at the AA and elsewhere. We did a good theme issue around one person, but with critical essays. That was in 1978. It corresponded to other themed issues that Andreas put together rather brilliantly.

HC: Historical ones.

CJ: Historical ones. I think I introduced him to Gavin Stamp and he did *Britain in the Thirties* and *Edwardian London*, which was really brilliant. Papadakis did a double issue on the Ecole des Beaux Arts. He got much of the text from the New York show at the Museum of Modern Art, and then got new people to write for it. That was a critical issue.

HC: The feeding of all of this material in and out of Post-Modernism is also quite critical. It created that excitement about historical styles.

CJ: And that approach brought history, in a polemical way, into the current discussion. There was an issue in 1979 on Alberti, which had a lot of good scholars in it. These are collectors' items and quality issues. If you want to know about the Beaux Arts or Alberti, read those issues. They have the standard of a book, or a very high-quality symposium. A little later, I introduced Andreas to Dimitri Porphyrios, who wrote *Modern Eclecticism*, an important book, and we got him into △D.[2] Dimitri and Andreas got on very well – as, indeed, he did with Leon and Rita Krier. Dimitri became a regular contributor. He published an issue in 1982, number 56, called *Classicism Is Not a Style*, in which he more or less attacked Post-Modernism and put forward a constructionist and symbolic view of classicism, which was much more revivalist than the free-style classicism that Post-Modernists were advocating. We managed to create a real debate, not just push one position.

HC: It was over a five-to six-year period that they were doing these historical issues?

CJ: In the mid-1980s, Catherine Cook produced historic issues on the Russian avant-garde that are very important. They contrast with the issues on the Beaux Arts, Bruce Goff and Alberti.

HC: It's interesting that those historical ones in a way were feeding into Post-Modernism, whereas hers were feeding into deconstruction.

CJ: That was the great thing about the 1980s. It really was

pluralist, so you could ring the changes; but each issue had its own integrity. Cook did the issue on the Russian avant-garde in 1983, and she followed it up with one on Chernikov in 1984. They kept alive certain ideas that had never been appreciated, except in Russia. It was cutting-edge thought on suppressed architecture. It did, as you say, feed into deconstruction, but it was also for itself – like other historical issues. △D had a high batting average. Out of six issues a year, you could say that, at the best of times, three or four would be collectors' items, and that is better than any other magazine; but maybe I'm prejudiced.

In 1984 Leon Krier also had a whole issue devoted to his polemic – which is extraordinary. In a sense, it was just a monograph on his work and drawings, guest-edited by Dimitri Porphyrios, with Leon's seductive drawings, very interesting urban theories and a strong critique of Modernist planning.

HC: That changed the whole way of thinking about cities, didn't it?

CJ: In this country, it was an important link with Jane Jacobs and her attack of 1961, *The Death and Life of Great American Cities*. This was taken up, in an architectural way, by Leon Krier and given architectural images. Yet his critique is very much like hers: in favour of mixed use, mixed planning and against the kind of zoning and separation of functions of Modernism. It proffers the 10-minute walking distance as the unit of the city, not the automobile, which was destroying the city. There was a lot in Leon's polemic that was taken up later by Prince Charles. By 1986, he'd more or less gone over to Leon's position. You have to remember that Prince Charles started as what was called a 'romantic pragmatist' and was in favour of Ted Cullinen's work and that sort of picturesque nationalism. Then he was persuaded by the 'Real Architecture Group' of John Simpson, and particularly Leon's writings and polemic – and maybe even this △D issue – to adopt Leon as an architect and leader. Then, of course, Leon broke away from Post-Modernism and, with Dimitri, became a very strict classicist.

I've often said that Leon Krier is just like Le Corbusier; he draws like Le Corbusier; he was a lover of Le Corbusier when young. He worked in Jim Stirling's office from 1975 to the early 1980s. He produced the monograph on Stirling and did many drawings for it.

Leon was a Post-Modernist in Jim Stirling's office until about 1981. I don't want to draw too strong a distinction, but by 1985 he had become a primitive classicist, and it's that issue of △ — 1978, number 54 — that is such a nice polemic. You could give that to the Prince and his minions, and they would see, yes, this is how to do the city. Leon put a cross through the bad examples of modern planning, just as Le Corbusier put a cross on what he didn't want and then redesigned them. Even in 1984, we can see how poetic and Post-Modern some of this work still is.

HC: So it's a year or so after this?

CJ: Three or four years after, and you find the deconstructionist argument. △ produced one issue after another – *Deconstruction 1, Deconstruction 2, Deconstruction 3* – and then they were collected in a big book of the three issues. Then came an issue called *Reconstruction Deconstruction: Peter Eisenman versus Leon Krier*. On the cover a polemical argument was presented with an Eisenman versus a Krier landscape. That's 1989. That was taking the polemic into the pages of △ so people could see what were the two leading movements: the reconstruction of the city, as Leon and Prince Charles were advocating, and the deconstruction of the city, as Eisenman was polemicising. In 1990-1 I wrote a book *The New Moderns*, discussing the shift away from Late Modernism into a kind of deconstruction. We produced several issues on the new moderns and the super moderns; for instance a critical issue called *The New Modern Aesthetic* in 1990, accompanied by several symposia. Then there was New Spirit in Architecture, 1991, which was a continuation of New Modernism. You can see that Andreas was picking up the avant-garde but I don't know whether, by that period, we were ahead of the game or simply following the avant-garde – above all, Daniel Libeskind, whose new Jewish Museum set the stage for Post-Modernism in the 1990s.

The 1990s and Fragmentation of the Architectural Culture
HC: Were you simply consolidating?

CJ: On deconstruction? I think the last thing that Andreas did was Theory and Experimentation which was, again, a symposium.[3] That one was connected to an exhibition on the top floor of Whiteleys. The book of the symposium, *Theory and Experimentation* included Libeskind, Mayne, Tschumi, Alsop, Coates, Decq, Domenig, Eisenman, Gehry, Hadid and just about everybody but Koolhaas, who wouldn't play ball. It was the beginning of coffee-table avant-gardism – or 'here comes everybody!'

LEON KRIER
HOUSES, PALACES, CITIES

Guest-Edited by Demetri Porphyrios

This issue of △ was an entire monograph devoted to Leon Krier's polemic, guest-edited by Demetri Porphyrios, *Architectural Design*, vol 54, no 7/8, 1984.

The New Modern Aesthetic

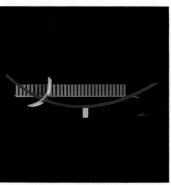

INTERNATIONAL SYMPOSIUM AT THE TATE GALLERY AND THE SECOND ANNUAL ARCHITECTURE FORUM
RICHARD MEIER • DANIEL LIBESKIND • CHARLES JENCKS

The *New Modern Aesthetic, Architectural Design*, vol 60, no 7/8, 1990

New Science = New Architecture,
Architectural Design, vol 67, no 9/10, 1997

HC: Going back, I think you identified several crucial turning points for architecture and *D*'s contribution to them: firstly, *The Language of Post-Modernism* and that period of review, after Late Modernism, of seriously looking at what had happened. That brought together things that had been going on since the late 1960s with Venturi – things in America. Then there was the important debate about urbanism. They all fed into the position that we are currently at now, which we tend to take for granted.

CJ: What happens is that you get a formation, a summary of position, and people then assume that is the status quo and the background for the next move. Architecture changes now every three or four years. But also it has these periods of quick focus. We are in another one now with a double focus – partly a neo-Minimalist period. Opposed to this is a wide movement that was present in the *New Science = New Architecture* issue of 1977 which I edited. This was on the new nonlinear sciences of complexity and it summarised one type of architecture of the year 2000 – stemming from Gehry, Eisenman, Libeskind, Koolhaas and Balmond the old avant garde – and that stemming from complexity theory and fractals (we published scientists). This wide movement also relates to cyberspace and hypersurface – what you call 'digital architecture'. These last are driven by technology and certain ideas of expression, rather more than deep philosophical ideas. They're not necessarily particularly architectural; they're more …

HC: They're more aesthetic in a way.

CJ: They're more aesthetic and experiential. They're important; the computer is extremely important. This is where magazine publishing is interesting. *D* must operate with the young turks who want to make their reputation, and they will come up through any marginal differentiation they can get. It may be cyberspace and film. In the last 10 years, *D* has not taken a particularly critical line. It has reflected what has been going on among creative young architects and published it, promoted it. In the 1960s, *D* was more critical of actual practice. From the 1970s, it was highly polemical. In the late 1970s and early 1980s it was Post-Modern and polemical, and then in the middle 1980s more classical. But since the 1990s, *D* has been more accepting of current trends.

HC: Do you think that reflects what's going on in architecture? There's a far wider acceptance of different trends. People are less critical.

CJ: That's right, and the Post-Modern pluralism has finally led to fragmentation where all approaches get a hearing.

HC: Anything goes.

CJ: Anything goes in the world of architectural publishing – the greatest amount of books, periodicals and weekly articles in history. A bonanza.

HC: People can sit back and appreciate different things.

CJ: Right, you've said it. In a consumer society there are fewer movements and more choices, a veritable department store of options, a series of *genres de vie*. So Minimalism has become, as it is in the boutiques, simply another style. Starting with iconoclasm, and in the 11th century as a spiritual and highly moral movement, it has now become a style of life. That is also true of cyberarchitecture: it's approaching a style. There is a danger. I believe that *D* must not only have a theoretical bent, but also a critical and polemical one. That has been its historical role. On the other hand, you could say, why shouldn't *D* just change, and change in any direction? It isn't standing still; it must respond quickly.

HC: It has to respond to what's going on.

CJ: And respond at the level of the students. Well, it does that, and it amplifies the *Zeitgeist*. But it needs a critical force. At least every fourth issue should be critical. We've done that with *Millennium Architecture*. It's philosophical and critical, and summarises what happened in 1999–2001, which is more than most writing on the millennium.

HC: That brings us up to date. *D*+

Charles Jencks' article 'The Bigness of Small Magazines', which further examines and resolves some of the issues raised here, will be featured in this section of the next issue of *D* (vol 71, no 1), *Young Blood*, guest-edited by Neil Spiller.

Practice Profile

Steve Tompkins (left) and Graham Haworth (right).

Haworth Tompkins

After less than a decade in practice, Haworth Tompkins has already made a visible impact on London's theatreland with its work on the Royal Court, Regent's Park Open Air Theatre and the Almeida's Gainsborough Studios. Edwin Heathcote sums up the partnership, whose output evokes a string of strong adjectives — 'tough', 'raw', 'muscled', 'rigorous'…

Gainsborough Studios for the Almeida Theatre, London, 2000.

London theatre suffocates under the weight of golden putti, plush velvet, garlanded domes and an atmosphere of snobby clubbishness. Over recent years, however, the London practice Haworth Tompkins has been instrumental in creating a layer between the frilly West End tourist traps and the bland modernity of the lottery-baby theatres. A number of recent theatrical projects, most notably the Royal Court (1999), have exposed Haworth Tompkins' work to a wide and appreciative public. Yet its lack of a self-congratulatory attitude, and its unwillingness to submit to the easy option of a single design 'style' within which to wrap all its works has led to its evolution into one of the most consistently interesting architectural practices on the London scene.

The tough but exquisitely thoughtful rebuilding of the Royal Court Theatre led the practice into a series of fascinating and diverse theatrical projects. From the industrial antichic of the Gainsborough Studios (2000) to the kitschy, tongue-in-cheek, fairy-grotto-stylings of the remodelled Regents Park Open Air Theatre (2000), the practice could easily have concentrated on the arts and made its Clerkenwell office into a comfortable, kissy-kissy, luvvy loft. Thankfully, it did not. The same robust rigour that it brought to its stripped-down theatres has been applied to a number of well-chosen commissions.

Haworth Tompkins' factory and office building for Doc Martens footwear in the English Midlands, close to the traditional bootville of Northampton (1996), is an essay in the kind of unfussy pragmatism for which Doc Martens has become so internationally recognisable. Its redevelopment of the seafront at Douglas on the Isle of Man (1998) displays a delicacy and finesse of detail that recalls the filigree frontages of Victorian promenades, while somehow entirely avoiding preciousness and

pastiche. A rhythmic elevation builds interest through a series of bays, balconies, setbacks and a sweeping, classic Modernist, curving corner treatment. The breezy facades pick up on a kind of 1930s nautical aesthetic evoking the classic era of Modernism, yet the vertical emphasis of bays and attenuated concrete fins anchors the building firmly to the ground and also into the local seaside context of the tall, narrow Victorian houses down the shore. Although more complex and, in many ways, more delicate, the Douglas seafront scheme built on the practice's first major commission, for an office complex in St Helier in Jersey (1996). Like the Douglas designs, the Jersey offices revolve around a curving corner treatment, here a glass cylinder containing the building's stairwells. The impeccable detailing and the rhythms of the two very different, but very modest, facades define the building's character.

Subtle elevational rhythms also form the basis of the designs for a major housing development in Coin Street (2000). Misleadingly simple and self-effacing, this scheme should provide one of the most critical elements in the tortuous and much-debated regeneration of London's South Bank, finally providing a firm community foundation for the arts and tourism through which the area thrives.

Trying to sum up the approach of a practice is like asking someone what kind of music they like. It might come out as a bit of jazz, a little urban, quite a bit of soul, perhaps quite a few classical and some modern works. In fact, in the case of Haworth Tompkins' approach to architecture, that's probably as fine a transposition as you could find. The best of its work seems to create bridges between opposing worlds, and the bridges themselves become places of profound contemplation from which the natures of both banks can be seen more clearly.

In the Royal Court, the practice managed to maintain the soul and the balls of the old theatre by stripping it naked and by revealing a kind of raw, muscled essence that creates a new, fascinating functioning environment without disposing of the sweaty, low-budget, backstage world of workshop theatre. In the Regent's Park Open Air Theatre, the eccentrically perverse English atmosphere of the ad hoc picnic and messing about outdoors in freezing, uncomfortable conditions was retained. The blend of fun and function is one that few architects can pull off without seeming excessively self-conscious. It demands a deep understanding with the clients, and a sense of humour which can so easily be squeezed out between the design and the building.

Along with this sense of humour comes a sense of humanity. Steve Tompkins says, 'It's about building a humanity into them – buildings do have parallel qualities to people. I think.' A blend of respect for the client and the history of the site, plus the willingness to question the brief and strip it down to its elements in order to preserve an essential character, defines all Haworth Tompkins' work. There is also an ever-present sense of theatricality. Not the luvvy-mwah-mwah kind you may expect from a practice so closely involved with the theatrical world, but a sense of the building as a stage; a series of dramatic details forming a broader narrative. To use a theatrical metaphor, this architecture is a blend of West End and workshop with the finesse and well-used experience of the former and the intense, functional fervour of the latter. Like the Royal Court itself, the architecture of Haworth Tompkins is concerned both with the radical and the poetic, with history and with a future that is ensured in one of the most profound theatre buildings to be constructed in London in the last 100 years.

The Royal Court Theatre, London, 1999

The enigma of London's most radical showcase for young writing, the birthplace of Kitchen Sink and Angry Young Men, is that it should exist in an utterly conventional Victorian theatre in the heart of London's swankiest shopping area. It was exactly this incongruity that Haworth Tompkins had to work with and maintain in its recent rebuilding of the theatre. In this fantastically delicate operation, respect for the building's history and the feel of the stage had to combine with huge rebuilding to include extensive new backstage and front-of-house facilities and a large restaurant and bar. The easy option would have been a complete reconstruction, perhaps behind the original facade. The route taken by Haworth Tompkins, however, was more akin to a kind of open-heart surgery: the beating heart of the scheme is the original auditorium. Much loved by performers and audiences, the theatre itself was retained but stripped back to its essentials. The frilly plasterwork of a postwar approximation of the Victorian original was ground down to reveal the tough, bolted iron plates of the structure, an industrial, almost non aesthetic, which seems to mirror the functional architecture of the underground that runs right next to the subterranean auditorium, its rumbling occasionally impinging on the quiet of the performance. To tighten the site further, and reinforce the surgical analogy, the architects also had to contend with the remains of the Cranbourne river, which now flows ingloriously next to the foundations through a sewer pipe and can be seen from the adjacent underground platforms.

Above top
New annex of the Royal Court Theatre.

Above bottom
Foyer.

Far left
Staircase with original brick wall revealed.

Left
Undercroft café.

Bounded by these tight site conditions, the architects expanded in the only two directions they could go: along the side of the theatre and beneath Sloane Square. The new facilities for backstage and administration were located in a long strip behind a curving Cor-ten screen, while a cavernous new restaurant/bar was created by burrowing beneath the road and the square. The result is a lofty subterranean space made rich through the use of dark, luscious timbers reclaimed from railway sleepers and old laboratory worktops, through exquisitely finished concrete and metal surfaces. It is the discovery of a new world beneath the too-expensive streets of Chelsea, yet the new world is tempered by solid and reused materials so that it seems to have aged like a wine-soaked barrel to create nuance and flavour in a space that never, somehow, feels new. The focus of this undercroft is the tantalising glimpse of bright crimson that leads the eye inexorably towards the auditorium. A curving plane (daubed in subtle red patterns by artist Antoni Malinowski) indicates the theatre's rear wall; this element rises through the building and is visible at all levels, from within and without, becoming a kind of cipher for the essential theatrical function of the complex. The red is echoed by the burning, simple neons of the elevation and its reflected glow creates a rather louche air, somehow suggesting the impossible dream of a fragment of Chelsea turning into a red-light district. Combine this with the new stairs to the undercroft doorway, carved from the old entrance to a Sloane Square public lavatory, and it completes the slightly dark, Ortonesque humour that is apparent throughout this complex, profound and thoughtful design.

Left
Original iron structure supporting upper circle of the Royal Court Theatre.

Above top
Coin Street Housing. In the background can be seen the London Eye.

Above
Model showing courtyard at Coin Street.

Opposite
Perspective of Coin Street Housing.

Coin Street Housing, South Bank, London, 2000

The South Bank – London's arts ghetto – is bounded by a disparate, often incoherent, series of urban situations, from the deadening office blocks of the 1970s to traffic-clogged roads and the Byzantine brick arches of the railway viaducts that punctuate the area. Haworth Tompkins' Coin Street development is an attempt to knit together some of the parts of that urban fabric into a coherent whole. The scheme grew out of the pioneering work of the Coin Street Community Builders, who were responsible for saving this part of the South Bank for low-cost residential units in the early 1980s when they were faced with the local population being squeezed out by big business interests and office development. Haworth Tompkins won the commission through a limited competition.

A U-shaped block encloses a garden and comprises 59 dwellings including 32 family houses for up to nine people. The scheme is built above car parking, which will help to subsidise the development, while the central communal garden, which will include playground facilities, supplements the small private gardens allocated to each house.

The architects have made a virtue of the length of the elevations by creating continuous brick walls that act like a kind of screen, which unifies the internal elements and creates a consistent language of openings but which also adds a kind of solidity and anchors the building in the brick tradition of this formerly industrial enclave. The elevations within the court are lightened by a series of screens and delicate balconies ensuring the residents maximum private exterior space. The enclosure of the courtyard will be completed by the next phase of the scheme, the Hothouse. This is planned as an educational and social centre for local residents and will be instrumental in training them for the kind of jobs now offered in the South Bank area; jobs in the arts, in administration and in services and retail. Architecturally the most striking part of the design, this final element represents an attempt to rejuvenate the street with an open, active elevation that will help to bind the fragmented urban fabric together.

Doc Martens HQ, Wollaston, 1996

Robust, thoughtful and with a fine eye for detail, Haworth Tompkins' factory and HQ for Doc Martens presages its later buildings, yet a boot factory could hardly seem further from the arts factories that now form such an important part of the architects' workload. A close-up view of the details of these solidly anchored buildings in Northamptonshire reveals that the distance is not as great as it may seem. The long, toplit factory spaces ground the building, a process that is helped along by earthy rather than high-tech materials. The language of super-tech would seem utterly inappropriate for what remains the essentially low-tech world of boot-and shoemaking, and Haworth Tompkins have approached the building with a blend of concentration on materials, generous spaces, good lighting and a sharp and logical delineation between spaces, functions and architectural elements in a tradition that stretches back into the pragmatic roots of Britain's industrial revolution.

From without, the building appears solid, robust and a little unforgiving. Inside, it looks thoughtful and well tailored, each junction and each material considered and existing for a reason. The prefabricated steel frames stand clearly separate from the stone cladding and the elevation of the roof above the walls creates an airy lightness, atypical of most industrial building. A double-height entrance space is clean and uncluttered. The subtle yet clear demarcation of elements within it is well demonstrated by the exquisite details of the stair, where it meets support and makes contact with the floor. Δ+

Major Works

1991   Practice founded

1993   Doc Martens Department Store, Covent Garden, London

1996   Doc Martens HQ, Wollaston, Northamptonshire
La Motte Street Offices, St Helier, Jersey

1997   House extension, London

1998   Loch Promenade, Douglas, Isle of Man, first phase

1999   Royal Court Theatre, London

2000   Gainsborough Studios, conversion into temporary performance space for the Almeida Theatre

       Regent's Park Open Air Theatre, remodelling of theatre and facilities

       Coin Street, Housing

       Royal Society of Arts, reorganisation

       Design for Ovingdean Performing Arts Centre for Deaf Children

Left
Main staircase of the
Doc Martens HQ.

Middle
Double-height entrance
to the factory.

Below
The Doc Martens HQ in construction.

Highlights from Wiley-Academy

THE TERRACOTTA DESIGNS OF ALFRED WATERHOUSE
Colin Cunningham

PB 0 471 48949 2; £34.95; 275 x 217 mm; 192 pages; November 2000

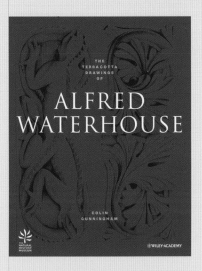

Love it or loathe it, the Natural History Museum is undoubtedly one of the most outstanding works of architecture to have emerged in the late Victorian period. Bursting with the confidence of the age, it is adorned with a range of ornament of which the enquiring eye can never tire, with terracotta likenesses of a variety of flora and fauna to match the richness of the contents of the museum. Both structure and ornament are the products of the mind of Alfred Waterhouse, whose painstaking work in designing every element is legendary. However, the importance of the building lies not only in the intricacy of the detail, but also in Waterhouse's decision to use terracotta for the implementation of the designs. In making this choice for such a prestigious building, he was flying in the face of convention by using a medium that had previously been regarded as inferior to the more respected and favoured medium of carved stone.

This book explains the development of the work of Waterhouse and the events that led to the designs for the Natural History Museum, as well as illustrating for the first time the beautiful drawings from which the ornamentation was executed. Although many of these were destroyed when their practical use had expired, over 130 still survive and are held in the museum's collection. Seldom seen and never before reproduced, they bear witness to the fact that Waterhouse was not only a skilled architect but also a highly accomplished draughtsman, who has been described as 'beyond question one of the most brilliant and facile' watercolour artists of his day. This book sets these designs in context as both works of art and specimens of scientific illustration, and provides an invaluable document of the work of an architect who influenced a generation at the end of the 19th century. ◬+

DESIGN PROFESSIONALS AND THE BUILT ENVIRONMENT Edited by Paul Knox and Peter Ozolins

HB 0 471 98515 5, £70; PB 0 471 98516 3, £24.95; 168 x 244 mm; 400 pages; November 2000

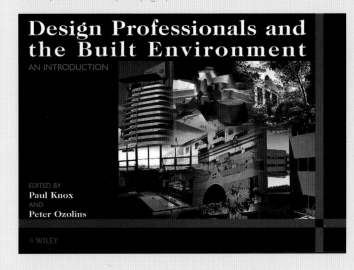

Until recently architects, building officials, planners, contractors and other practitioners in fields related to the built environment have learned the tools of their trade within specifically constructed professional boundaries, and have gone about their business as if their work existed in isolation from a wider professional and social context. But this is changing. The demands of today's market for property development and site planning necessitate communication – and even shared knowledge – between the professions. This need is being met by new professional and academic courses that aim to teach students in a more synthetic manner.

Design Professionals and the Built Environment is a tool for better work in this field. It introduces the range of issues involved in the analysis, design and production of the built environment, emphasising the interaction between them. With contributors and case material drawn from around the world, it provides a fully international account. Within the context of this comprehensive study, two key issues are given particular emphasis: information technology and the protection of our natural heritage. The rapid development of computer technology has enabled built environment professionals to gain access to an ever-increasing information base, which can then be dealt with in many more ways; yet the impact of this is not properly understood. Similarly, the impact of the world's six billion inhabitants on the natural environment is clearly critical, but by and large does not inform the actions of most design professionals. Through pointing to the experiences of others from which we can learn, this book encourages students to take a more holistic approach to the planning and design of the built environment. ◬+

Book Review

THE GREEN SKYSCRAPER – The Basis for
Designing Sustainable Intensive Buildings,
by Ken Yeang, Prestel Verlag (Munich) 1999

This is an invaluable guide to designing dwellings for the vertical expansion of urban form. It is absolutely essential for anyone involved in urban development. Not only will it alter perceptions about skyscrapers, but will also be a fundamental preparation for a future that we have forced upon ourselves. *The Green Skyscraper* is a call to the design community to create ecologically responsive urban towers, as well as an indispensable step-by-step guide on how to actually do it.

Ken Yeang acknowledges the fact that nature is not something separate from the human species, even in the urban context, and that our environment must now take into account man-made systems as part of its ecology. The physical existence of the skyscraper will affect the environment, as does the daily functioning of the systems within the building. Buildings act as living organisms, consuming energy and producing output in the same way as animals and other ecosystems.

Yeang begins with a particularly convincing argument as to why large towers and centralised land-use are potentially advantageous to our species, whilst recognising that current skyscrapers are indeed detrimental to the environment. He defines a skyscraper as any building over 10 storeys high and stresses its value as a solution to the challenge of increased density, since almost half the world's population now lives in urban environments.

He distinguishes ecological design as a system that can be energy productive as well as healing to a damaged environment. He challenges the design community to take responsibility for the development of our cities and to create buildings that are fully integrated into the surrounding ecosystems. His holistic analysis of the benefits of ecologically designed skyscrapers begins to make perfect sense, and this is meticulously illustrated through various charts and diagrams.

By chapter two, Yeang outlines a definitive point-by-point manifesto for ecological design that could be applied to any built structure from a garden shed to an urban development. Chapter three expands on this by presenting a theory of ecological design as a law that is represented as a matrix with four types of interaction: external interdependencies, internal interdependencies, system inputs and system outputs. He explains that a designer should consider each of these factors. Failure to do so could result in an unbalanced design.

This matrix represents a model that can be effectively used by the architect and other disciplines involved in analysing ecological impacts, to create 'multiple comprehensiveness'. With each field following the same frame of reference, all environmental interactions will be covered and a strategy to deal with issues can be harmoniously created.

Although he defines this as a law, Yeang also makes it clear that the interactions framework must not be a substitute for design invention. His approach to various processes is as organic and open-ended as the ecological systems with which he is concerned.

The succeeding chapters provide a guide on how to design an ecological building, beginning with a completely integrated and environmentally conscious assessment of what exactly needs to be built. The next step is to look at the ecosystem of the actual building site before any actions are taken. The subsequent decisions must then account for any off-site impacts on the environment.

By chapter seven, Yeang gets into the design of the skyscraper's operational systems. This is where he presents information on the technology necessary for achieving a green skyscraper. Many possibilities are covered, including utilising passive design for heating, lighting and ventilation as well as innovative ideas for vertical landscaping.

Yeang recognises the complexities involved in ecological design and believes that the design process should be a form of applied ecology in itself. He presents a variety of methods and models for analysing and designing ecological buildings, as he defines the procedure as both prognostic and anticipatory.

Yeang's research is straightforward and his descriptions of the problems present viable solutions. His sensitive and comprehensive insight into the environment and the urban form is representative of someone who has taken an exceptionally profound step to change the way in which we build our cities.

The Green Skyscraper touches on the spiritual, philosophical, scientific and artistic aspects of urban sustainability whilst being firmly rooted in the practicalities of building ecological towers in the present. Yeang is not a naive idealist but a sensible visionary. Although it is aimed at architects and those in the building industry, this book is accessible to anyone with an interest in solutions for a sustainable planet. The ideas could essentially be applied to any functioning system from computers to personal physiology, since they are models applicable to any level of human interaction with the natural environment. As important to the future of ecological design as D'Arcy Thompson's *Biomorphic Growth of Form*, *The Green Skyscraper* is well written and vigilantly researched by a significant architect who is attempting to take a lead in saving our planet. *Δ*+ *Chris McCarthy*

Steven Gartside takes a wider look at the area surrounding Michael Wilford's highly praised Lowry Centre in Salford.

In the consumption of cultural sites – particularly those in which architecture and contents aim to compete for equal status – the journey to them should be a mere transitory fragment, ready to become lost in the wider experience. Yet to visit Michael Wilford's new Lowry Centre is to be reminded of the importance of space and place. There is a confusion of identity on the site, something that can often occur with schemes that are part of regeneration packages.

This new cultural building lies in a non-place on the side of the Manchester Ship Canal between the desperate and declining Salford and a busy Manchester trying to reinvent itself as a vibrant European city. The site was always going to make the Lowry Centre an outstanding piece of architecture: it sits in the midst of a business and leisure theme park whose sheer banality is infinitely reproduced in the reflective facades of the surrounding office boxes. It is all too easy to criticise the crass commercialism of quick-build office and leisure spaces. The Lowry Centre and, facing it across the water, Daniel Libeskind's Imperial War Museum are able to be separated out because they are part of the rich vein of lottery-funded cultural projects. What has occurred on this Manchester/ Salford site is reliance on two high-profile cultural projects to allow for a further commercial regeneration.

When viewers come out of the Lowry Centre they are confronted by a multistorey car park and the familiar multi-use complex containing shops, health club, cinema, bars, restaurants, etc. The mall or arcade has been around since the mid-19th century, and has been studied in its various historical manifestations since Walter Benjamin's work of the 1930s. The idea then, is nothing new: the mall or arcade relies on being a space that is complete within itself or a place of difference or refuge from what surrounds it. When a site is outside an urban area and is being developed for many different projects, issues of controlled and careful planning can often be lost. This leads to a fragmented body of buildings, each trying to be complete within themselves but uncertain as to their relationship to the wider whole.

But, back to the journey itself, because it is the journey that is symptomatic of the problems inherent in the site. For visitors separated from their cars, the Metrolink is designed to provide a fast and efficient urban/city transport system – and it does, until it reaches the edge of Salford Quays where bad planning means that the track curves and winds so much in between buildings that the metro slows to a virtual crawl. This last slow section of the journey provides an overemphasis on the 1980s legacy of city-edge office building, punctuated by chain fast-food restaurants – inside of which, uniformed, minimum-wage recruits try to keep up the strained surface of the simulated environment of service culture.

The journey to the Lowry Centre should act as a marker or warning of the significant dangers that can arise when space and place are not adequately considered. Rather than trying to define areas of public space that are able to give a relaxed coherence to an area, there is a reliance on the repeated reworking of the mini-malls. The success or failure of cultural sites is dependent on a thriving multiplicity; the spaces that surround them need to be given the importance of the content consumed. ◠+

Steven Gartside teaches on the MA Programme at Tate Gallery, Liverpool, and is currently working on the exhibition '(Dis)integration: Architecture/ Sculpture' for the Henry Moore Institute, Leeds.

Subscribe Now for 2001

As an influential and prestigious architectural publication, *Architectural Design* has an almost unrivalled reputation worldwide. Published bi-monthly as six individual titles, it successfully combines the currency and topicality of a newsstand journal with the editorial rigour and design qualities of a book. Consistently at the forefront of cultural thought and design since the 60s, it has time and again proved provocative and inspirational — inspiring theoretical, creative and technological advances. Prominent in the 80s for the part it played in Post-Modernism and then in Deconstruction, ⚎ has recently taken a pioneering role in the technological revolution of the 90s. With ground-breaking titles dealing with cyberspace and hypersurface architecture, it has pursued the conceptual and critical implications of high-end computer software and virtual realities. ⚎

⚎ Architectural Design

SUBSCRIPTION RATES 2001
Institutional Rate: UK £150
Personal Rate: UK £97
Student* Rate: UK £70
OUTSIDE UK
Institutional Rate: US $225
Personal Rate: US $145
Student* Rate: US $105

*Proof of studentship will be required when placing an order. Prices reflect rates for a 2001 subscription and are subject to change without notice.

TO SUBSCRIBE
Phone your credit card order:
UK/Europe: +44 (0)1243 843 828
USA: +1 212 850 6645
Fax your credit card order to:
UK/Europe: +44 (0)1243 770 432
USA: +1 212 850 6021

Email your credit card order to:
cs-journals@wiley.co.uk
Post your credit card or cheque order to:

UK/Europe: John Wiley & Sons Ltd.
Journals Administration Department
1 Oldlands Way
Bognor Regis
West Sussex PO22 9SA
UK

USA: John Wiley & Sons Ltd.
Journals Administration Department
605 Third Avenue
New York, NY 10158
USA

Please include your postal delivery address with your order.

All ⚎ volumes are available individually. To place an order please write to:
John Wiley & Sons Ltd
Customer Services
1 Oldlands Way
Bognor Regis
West Sussex PO22 9SA

Please quote the ISBN number of the issue(s) you are ordering.

○ I wish to subscribe to ⚎ Architectural Design at the **Institutional rate.**

○ I wish to subscribe to ⚎ Architectural Design at the **Personal rate.**

○ I wish to subscribe to ⚎ Architectural Design at the **Student rate.**

STARTING FROM ISSUE 1/2001.

○ Payment enclosed by Cheque/Money order/Drafts.

Value/Currency £/US$ [　　　　]

○ Please charge £/US$ [　　　　] to my credit card.

Account number:

[ ][ ][ ][ ][ ][ ][ ][ ][ ][ ][ ][ ][ ][ ][ ][ ]

Expiry date:

[ ][ ][ ][ ][ ]

Card: Visa/Amex/Mastercard/Eurocard *(delete as applicable)*

Cardholder's signature [　　　　　　　]

Cardholder's name [　　　　　　　]

Address [　　　　　　　]

[　　　　　　　]

[　　　　] Post/Zip Code [　　　]

Recepient's name [　　　　　　　]

Address [　　　　　　　]

[　　　　　　　]

[　　　　] Post/Zip Code [　　　]

I am interested in the following Back Issues at £19.99 each:

○ ⚎ 147 *The Tragic in Architecture*, Richard Patterson

○ ⚎ 146 *The Transformable House*, Jonathan Bell and Sally Godwin

○ ⚎ 145 *Contemporary Processes in Architecture*, Ali Rahim

○ ⚎ 144 *Space Architecture*, Dr Rachel Armstrong

○ ⚎ 143 *Architecture and Film II*, Bob Fear

○ ⚎ 142 *Millennium Architecture*, Maggie Toy and Charles Jencks

○ ⚎ 141 *Hypersurface Architecture II*, Stephen Perrella

○ ⚎ 140 *Architecture of the Borderlands*, Teddy Cruz

○ ⚎ 139 *Minimal Architecture II*, Maggie Toy

○ ⚎ 138 *Sci-Fi Architecture*, Maggie Toy

○ ⚎ 137 *Des-Res Architecture*, Maggie Toy

○ ⚎ 136 *Cyberspace Architecture II*, Neil Spiller

○ ⚎ 135 *Ephemeral/Portable Architecture*, Robert Kronenburg

○ ⚎ 134 *The Everyday and Architecture*, Sarah Wigglesworth

○ ⚎ 133 *Hypersurface Architecture*, Stephen Perrella

○ ⚎ 132 *Tracing Architecture*, Nikos Georgiadis

○ ⚎ 131 *Consuming Architecture*, Sarah Chaplin and Eric Holding